Essential Malta

A Whirlwind Tour of Malta's Rich Heritage

Introduction to Malta - The Island of Wonders

Nestled in the heart of the sparkling Mediterranean Sea, Malta stands as a captivating island of wonders, a place where history, culture, and natural beauty intertwine in a harmonious embrace. This small archipelago, located south of Sicily, boasts a rich tapestry of tales that stretch back through millennia, leaving an indelible mark on the world's historical stage.

With a land area of just 316 square kilometers, Malta may appear diminutive on a map, but its significance surpasses its size. The islands that comprise Malta – Malta itself, Gozo, and Comino – form a unique tapestry of landscapes, from rugged cliffs and pristine beaches to rolling hills adorned with charming villages. Each corner of this enchanting paradise unfolds a new chapter of history, making it a true gem for travelers and history enthusiasts alike.

Malta's history is as intricate as the mosaic tiles found in its ancient temples. It was a crucible of civilizations, witnessing the rise and fall of empires and becoming a strategic outpost for seafarers throughout the ages. Phoenicians, Carthaginians, Romans, Arabs, Normans, and others have all left their footprints on this blessed land. However, the chapter that stands out most vividly is the legacy of the Knights Hospitaller, better known as the Knights of St. John, who arrived in the 16th century and established their stronghold on the island.

The architectural wonders that adorn Malta's landscape are a testament to its rich history. The medieval city of Mdina, with its honey-hued stone walls and narrow cobblestone streets, exudes an old-world charm that transports visitors back in time. Equally captivating is Valletta, the capital city, a UNESCO World Heritage Site and a living testament to the artistic prowess of the Knights. Its magnificent Baroque palaces, fortifications, and grand churches bear witness to the island's significance during the Renaissance era.

Beyond its historical significance, Malta offers a feast for the senses through its vibrant culture and heartwarming hospitality. The Maltese people are renowned for their warm, welcoming nature, eager to share their traditions and customs with visitors. Festivals and religious celebrations color the island's calendar throughout the year, infusing the atmosphere with joy and reverence. The Maltese Carnival, a boisterous affair of masks and revelry, adds a touch of merriment to the island's cultural tapestry.

Maltese cuisine is a delightful blend of Mediterranean flavors, reflecting its diverse heritage. From fresh seafood dishes that pay homage to its maritime past to hearty stews that harken back to rustic village traditions, every meal becomes a celebration of local produce and culinary expertise. Savory pastizzi, delicate rabbit dishes, and decadent desserts like kannoli tempt the taste buds, leaving a lasting impression on food enthusiasts who embark on a culinary journey across the island.

Malta's natural wonders are no less impressive than its cultural heritage. Its azure waters invite visitors to explore an underwater world brimming with marine life and mesmerizing shipwrecks, making it a diver's paradise. The picturesque Blue Lagoon on the island of Comino entices sun-seekers with its crystal-clear waters, while the rugged coastline offers breathtaking views and secluded coves for those seeking tranquility.

As the Maltese sun casts a warm glow over its shores, visitors cannot help but be drawn to the magnetic allure of this island of wonders. Whether exploring ancient temples, reliving epic battles, savoring local delicacies, or basking in the natural splendor, Malta has a way of captivating the heart and leaving an indelible impression that lasts a lifetime. With its rich history, diverse culture, and awe-inspiring landscapes, Malta stands as a testament to the human spirit's ingenuity and the timeless allure of this enchanting island nation. So, come, embark on a journey of discovery, for Malta awaits, ready to share its wonders with all who seek its embrace.

Unraveling Malta's Rich History - From Ancient Civilizations to Modern Times

In the heart of the Mediterranean lies the captivating island of Malta, steeped in a history as rich and diverse as the lands it occupies. From ancient civilizations to modern times, Malta's story unfolds like a tapestry woven with threads of conquest, trade, and cultural exchange.

The earliest traces of human habitation on Malta date back to around 5200 BC, during the Neolithic period. The island's prehistoric temples, such as the UNESCO-listed sites of Ġgantija on Gozo and Ħaġar Qim on Malta, stand as a testament to the island's ancient heritage. These megalithic structures, believed to be some of the world's oldest freestanding stone buildings, offer a glimpse into the religious and architectural practices of Malta's first inhabitants.

Over the centuries, Malta became a melting pot of civilizations due to its strategic location in the Mediterranean. Phoenicians, Carthaginians, and Romans each left their mark, introducing trade, agriculture, and Roman governance to the island. However, it was the Arabs who arrived in the 9th century that significantly influenced Malta's language and culture, leaving a lasting impact on the Maltese identity.

The medieval era heralded a new chapter in Malta's history with the arrival of the Normans, who conquered the island in the 11th century. Their rule was followed by that of the Swabians and the Angevins, before the island fell under the control of the Aragonese Crown of Sicily. However, it was the year 1530 that marked a turning point when Charles V of Spain granted the island to the Knights Hospitaller, who sought refuge from the invading Ottoman Empire.

Under the Knights' rule, Malta flourished as a hub of chivalry and culture. The fortified city of Valletta, named after Grand Master Jean Parisot de Valette, was built and remains a living monument to the Knights' grandeur and architectural prowess. The Knights' noble heritage is evident in the majestic buildings and churches that dot the city's skyline, such as St. John's Co-Cathedral, adorned with intricate Baroque art and the famed painting "The Beheading of Saint John the Baptist" by Caravaggio.

Yet, Malta's history also bears witness to the Great Siege of 1565, when the Knights valiantly defended the island against the Ottoman forces led by Suleiman the Magnificent. This epic battle, lasting for several months, saw the Maltese and the Knights stand united in the face of overwhelming odds, emerging victorious and solidifying Malta's position as a symbol of resistance against the Ottoman Empire.

In the 19th century, Malta became a British colony, and its strategic importance as a naval base was reinforced during World War I and World War II. The island played a pivotal role as a supply and support hub for the British Mediterranean Fleet, enduring heavy bombardments during the latter conflict, which earned it the George Cross for bravery and resilience.

The post-war era witnessed Malta's journey to independence, finally achieved in 1964. Despite its small size, the island nation took bold steps in shaping its destiny, joining the European Union in 2004 and adopting the euro as its currency in 2008. Today, Malta stands as a vibrant and modern nation, known for its thriving economy, welcoming people, and a commitment to preserving its cultural heritage.

The Maltese Archipelago - Geography and Unique Natural Features

Nestled in the azure waters of the Mediterranean Sea, the Maltese Archipelago comprises three main islands: Malta, Gozo, and Comino. Despite their small size, these islands boast a diverse and enchanting geography, making them a truly extraordinary destination for travelers and nature enthusiasts alike.

The largest of the three islands, Malta, covers an area of 246 square kilometers and is home to the majority of the country's population. Its landscape is a captivating blend of rolling hills, fertile valleys, and rugged cliffs, each offering a unique perspective of the island's beauty. The island's coastline stretches for approximately 196 kilometers, providing ample opportunities for visitors to explore its stunning beaches, hidden coves, and natural harbors.

Gozo, the second-largest island, measures approximately 67 square kilometers and is characterized by a more rural and tranquil setting compared to its bustling sister island. Known as the "Island of Calypso" from Greek mythology, Gozo's landscape is adorned with fertile farmlands, quaint villages, and impressive coastal cliffs. Its idyllic countryside beckons visitors to immerse themselves in its serene and picturesque surroundings.

The smallest of the trio, Comino, is a true gem of the Mediterranean, covering just 3.5 square kilometers. Despite its size, Comino's natural beauty is unparalleled, attracting visitors with its crystal-clear waters and unspoiled landscapes. The island's renowned Blue Lagoon is a mesmerizing turquoise oasis that invites travelers to relax in its pristine waters and soak up the sun amidst the rugged, limestone cliffs.

One of the most distinctive features of the Maltese Archipelago is its geology, with its limestone formations dating back millions of years. The islands are formed primarily from coralline limestone, which has been sculpted by nature over millennia, giving rise to the mesmerizing cliffs and intriguing rock formations that dot the landscape. The geological makeup of the islands also contributes to the formation of numerous caves and grottoes, offering explorers an opportunity to delve into the secrets of the underground world.

Malta's geology has also given rise to the fascinating phenomenon of karst topography. The island's porous limestone allows rainwater to permeate the ground, creating an intricate network of underground channels and reservoirs. The result is a scarcity of surface water bodies, making the country almost entirely dependent on groundwater resources for its freshwater needs.

Amidst the limestone landscape, Malta is also adorned with verdant valleys that offer a stark contrast to the arid terrain. These fertile valleys, known as "wieds" in Maltese, are a testament to the island's ability to support agriculture, despite its limited water resources. The ingenuity of the Maltese people in harnessing every drop of rainwater through a system of water catchment and distribution known as "għajn," further enhances the islands' unique ecological and cultural identity.

Beyond its terrestrial features, the Maltese Archipelago also boasts a vibrant marine ecosystem. The surrounding Mediterranean waters are teeming with marine life, providing a haven for colorful fish, dolphins, and even the endangered loggerhead sea turtles. Diving enthusiasts flock to the islands to explore their numerous underwater caves, reefs, and ancient shipwrecks, which are now thriving artificial reefs supporting marine biodiversity.

The Maltese People - An Insight into Their Customs and Traditions

At the heart of the Maltese Archipelago beats the spirit of its warm and welcoming people, who have woven a tapestry of customs and traditions that enrich the cultural fabric of this enchanting nation. The Maltese people, known for their hospitality and strong sense of community, embrace a way of life that cherishes family ties, celebrates festivity, and preserves their unique identity.

Family is the cornerstone of Maltese society, and the ties that bind extend beyond immediate kin to encompass extended family and close friends. Multigenerational households, where grandparents, parents, and children live under one roof, foster strong bonds and a deep sense of belonging. Family gatherings are cherished occasions, with food, laughter, and storytelling forming the foundation of these joyous events.

Hospitality is an intrinsic part of the Maltese way of life. Visitors are welcomed with open arms and treated to an abundance of food and drink, showcasing the generosity and warmth of the Maltese people. It is common to find a table laden with traditional delicacies, such as pastizzi (flaky pastries filled with ricotta or peas), timpana (baked pasta dish), and ftira (a local bread), all lovingly prepared to share the flavors of Malta with guests.

Religion plays a significant role in the lives of the Maltese people, with the majority of the population adhering to Roman Catholicism. The island is dotted with beautiful churches and chapels, each representing a spiritual anchor for the communities they serve. Religious festivals are a cherished tradition, with vibrant processions and colorful celebrations taking place throughout the year, especially during the feast of the patron saint of each village.

The Maltese people take great pride in preserving their cultural heritage, and traditional crafts are a testament to their craftsmanship and creativity. Talented artisans pass down skills from one generation to the next, ensuring that traditional crafts, such as lace-making (bizzilla), pottery (għażiż), and metalwork (kannizzati), continue to thrive. Local markets, like the Marsaxlokk Fish Market, showcase a fusion of tradition and modernity, offering a glimpse into the vibrant market culture that has evolved over the centuries.

Folklore and superstitions are woven into the daily lives of the Maltese people, adding a touch of mystique and charm to their customs. It is believed that the "kangli" (evil eye) can bring misfortune, and as a protective measure, many homes and businesses display talismans or red objects to ward off its effects. Festivals and celebrations are often accompanied by folk dances and music, which have been handed down through generations and provide a colorful window into the island's cultural heritage.

The Maltese language, Maltese (Il-Lingwa Maltija), is the only Semitic language in the European Union and reflects the island's diverse history and influences. A unique blend of Arabic, Italian, and English elements, Maltese serves as a living linguistic treasure, preserving the island's identity and acting as a bridge between its past and present.

Modern Maltese society has embraced globalization while preserving its cultural roots, leading to a harmonious fusion of old and new. Festivals, such as Carnival and the Malta International Arts Festival, celebrate artistic expression and creativity, showcasing the evolving cultural landscape of the island. Music, too, plays a vital role, with traditional folk songs and contemporary genres finding a place in the hearts of the Maltese people.

Maltese Cuisine - A Gastronomic Adventure of Flavors

Embark on a culinary journey through the vibrant world of Maltese cuisine, where flavors intertwine like the threads of a rich tapestry, weaving together a delightful gastronomic adventure. From traditional recipes handed down through generations to modern interpretations that embrace innovation, Maltese cuisine reflects the island's diverse history and the bounty of its fertile lands and surrounding seas.

At the heart of Maltese cuisine lies a celebration of fresh, locally sourced ingredients that pay homage to the island's agricultural heritage. The Maltese soil yields an abundance of produce, including sun-kissed tomatoes, succulent olives, fragrant herbs like basil and thyme, and the island's signature vegetable, the humble and versatile ġbejna (goat cheese). These ingredients form the foundation of many Maltese dishes, ensuring that each meal is a delightful burst of natural flavors.

Seafood holds a special place in Maltese hearts, given the island's maritime traditions. The waters surrounding Malta teem with a diverse array of fish, including lampuki (dolphin fish), swordfish, and tuna, making fish a staple of the Maltese diet. Grilled or stewed with locally grown capers and tomatoes, fish dishes embody the essence of Mediterranean flavors and are a testament to the island's culinary prowess.

As the sun sets over the island, the aroma of pastizzi fills the air, enticing passersby with its flaky pastry and delectable fillings. These savory pastries, often stuffed with ricotta cheese or a mixture of peas and onions, have become a quintessential Maltese street food, enjoyed by locals and visitors alike. Their origins can be traced back to Arab influence during the island's history, showcasing the rich tapestry of cultures that have left their mark on Maltese cuisine.

For those seeking a taste of the sea, Maltese fish soup, known as aljotta, is a hearty and flavorful dish that warms the soul. Made with fresh fish, tomatoes, garlic, and a dash of local saffron, this aromatic soup is a reminder of Malta's Mediterranean roots and its love affair with the sea.

The Maltese take great pride in their traditional stews, known as "bragioli" and "laham fuq il-fwar," each offering a comforting and satisfying experience. Bragioli features thin slices of beef rolled and stuffed with a mixture of bacon, onions, and hard-boiled eggs, simmered in a tomato-based sauce. Laham fuq il-fwar, on the other hand, is a slow-cooked lamb stew infused with wine and a medley of herbs and spices, creating a tender and flavorful masterpiece.

Maltese ftira, a circular bread with a crusty exterior and a soft, chewy center, is a culinary delight that has captured the hearts of locals for centuries. Served as an accompaniment to meals or stuffed with a variety of fillings like tuna, capers, olives, and fresh vegetables, the ftira embodies the spirit of Maltese simplicity and the joy of savoring quality ingredients.

Desserts in Malta are a decadent affair, with delights such as kannoli, honey-drenched pastries known as imqaret, and the popular figolli stealing the show. Figolli, almond-filled pastry shaped like symbolic figures, are enjoyed during

Easter, adding a touch of sweetness to the island's religious festivities.

As a melting pot of cultures, Maltese cuisine also boasts a range of delectable sweet and savory pastries, influenced by Italian, Arabic, and British traditions. This fusion of flavors showcases the island's openness to embracing culinary influences from afar while adding its distinctive Maltese twist.

With a culinary heritage deeply rooted in tradition and an openness to culinary innovation, Malta's gastronomic adventure invites travelers and food enthusiasts to savor a world of flavors. From humble street food to elaborate feasts, each dish serves as a culinary gateway to the heart and soul of this enchanting island. So, take a seat at the Maltese table, where every bite is a celebration of history, culture, and the joy of savoring life's simple pleasures.

Malta's Wildlife - A Diverse Ecosystem Amidst the Mediterranean

In the embrace of the sparkling Mediterranean Sea lies Malta, a tiny archipelago that boasts a remarkably diverse ecosystem teeming with unique wildlife. Despite its small size, Malta's biodiversity is a treasure trove of natural wonders, where an array of terrestrial and marine species have found a sanctuary amidst the sun-kissed shores and rugged landscapes.

Malta's avian inhabitants are a source of fascination for ornithologists and nature enthusiasts alike. As a vital migratory route for birds traveling between Europe and Africa, the islands serve as a crucial rest stop for various bird species during their arduous journeys. The majestic White Stork, Lesser Kestrel, and European Bee-eater are just a few of the migratory birds that grace the Maltese skies, delighting observers with their aerial acrobatics and vibrant plumage.

Of particular interest is Malta's national bird, the Blue Rock Thrush, locally known as il-Merill. With its striking blue coloration and melodious song, this resident bird has become an emblem of the island's unique wildlife. Other indigenous avian species, such as the Maltese Sparrow and the Spectacled Warbler, add to the island's avian diversity, each contributing to the vibrant symphony of nature that fills the Maltese countryside.

Malta's coastal waters host a thriving marine ecosystem, brimming with an array of marine life. From colorful fish to majestic cetaceans, the waters surrounding the islands offer a mesmerizing underwater world for divers and snorkelers to explore. The posidonia meadows, a unique underwater plant habitat, act as vital nurseries for juvenile fish and provide shelter for a myriad of marine organisms, further enriching the island's biodiversity.

Sea turtles, such as the loggerhead and green turtle, are a rare and precious sight in the Mediterranean, yet Malta remains one of the few places where these gentle giants can still be found. Protected nesting sites, such as Golden Bay and Ramla Bay, are essential for the conservation of these endangered species, offering a glimmer of hope for their survival in the region.

Delving into the underwater depths, divers may encounter the vibrant posidonia meadows, which act as vital nurseries for juvenile fish and provide shelter for a myriad of marine organisms, further enriching the island's biodiversity. The seagrass meadows also play a significant role in carbon sequestration, helping to mitigate the impact of climate change on marine ecosystems.

Malta's rocky shores are home to a variety of fascinating marine creatures, such as the elusive Mediterranean Moray Eel and the spiny Devilfish. These remarkable underwater dwellers, along with colorful octopuses and inquisitive groupers, add a touch of intrigue to the island's aquatic realm.

The Maltese islands are also blessed with an array of endemic plants, which are found nowhere else in the world. The Maltese Rock Centaury (Centaurium maritimum) and the Maltese Sea Lavender (Limonium melitense) are just two examples of the island's unique floral heritage, each contributing to the delicate balance of its natural ecosystems.

While Malta's rich biodiversity is a testament to its ecological resilience, it is not without challenges. As an island nation experiencing urbanization and tourism growth, conservation efforts are vital to protect its delicate ecosystems and ensure the survival of its diverse wildlife.

Malta's commitment to nature conservation is evident through the establishment of nature reserves and protected areas, such as the Majjistral Nature and History Park and the Island of Filfla. These sanctuaries provide vital habitats for endangered species and serve as educational centers for visitors and locals alike, fostering a deeper understanding and appreciation of Malta's natural heritage.

Delving into Malta's Folklore and Festivities

Step into the enchanting world of Malta's folklore and festivities, where age-old traditions and mythical tales converge in a joyous celebration of culture and community. The Maltese people hold these customs close to their hearts, cherishing the legacy of their ancestors and passing down their rich heritage to future generations.

Folklore weaves a captivating tapestry of legends, beliefs, and superstitions that have shaped the Maltese way of life for centuries. One such folklore centers around the "Luzzu," the traditional brightly painted fishing boats that dot the harbors of Malta. Believed to bring luck and protect fishermen from the perils of the sea, these eye-catching boats bear the iconic "Eye of Osiris," a symbol of protection against the evil eye, a belief that has its roots in ancient cultures.

Myths and legends permeate the Maltese landscape, adding a touch of mystique to the island's geography. The megalithic temples, such as Ġgantija and Ħaġar Qim, are believed to be the handiwork of giants, while the network of mysterious cart ruts etched into the rocky terrain continues to puzzle archaeologists and locals alike. These enigmatic features have given rise to countless tales, passed down through generations, that imbue Malta's ancient sites with an air of magic and wonder.

Throughout the year, Malta comes alive with a calendar brimming with festive celebrations that unite communities and showcase the island's vibrant spirit. Religious feasts are an integral part of Maltese culture, each village celebrating its patron saint with fervor and splendor. Lavish processions wind through the streets, accompanied by traditional brass bands playing solemn hymns and joyful tunes, while fireworks light up the night sky in a breathtaking display of reverence and joy.

The Carnival of Malta, celebrated in the week leading up to Lent, transforms the island into a riot of color, music, and revelry. Dazzling costumes, elaborate floats, and exuberant parades fill the streets, as locals and visitors alike embrace the spirit of Carnival with boundless enthusiasm. This age-old tradition offers a brief respite from the solemnity of Lent, inviting all to immerse themselves in the joy of celebration and camaraderie.

The Feast of St. Paul's Shipwreck stands as one of Malta's most cherished religious events, commemorating the shipwreck of the Apostle Paul on the island. Held on February 10th, the feast brings together diverse communities in a harmonious display of devotion and unity. The festivities include religious processions, music, and dance, as well as a unique tradition of horse races along the capital city's streets, an event that dates back to the 16th century.

Traditional Maltese weddings are a true testament to the island's rich folklore. The bride's gown, a masterpiece of handcrafted lace, is passed down through generations, symbolizing continuity and family ties. The groom wears a waistcoat adorned with silver filigree buttons, a tradition that dates back to the time of the Knights. Guests shower the couple with rice, symbolizing fertility and prosperity, adding a touch of traditional charm to this joyous occasion.

Music and dance are intrinsic to Malta's folklore, with traditional folk songs and dances weaving a musical tapestry that reflects the island's history and cultural influences. The "Għana," a form of improvised folk singing, captivates audiences with its heartfelt emotions and poignant tales. The "Farruġa," a lively folk dance, showcases the rhythmic energy and joie de vivre of the Maltese people, inviting all to join in the revelry and celebration.

Language in Malta - An Exploration of Maltese, English, and Other Influences

In the heart of the Mediterranean Sea, the island nation of Malta is home to a linguistic tapestry that reflects the island's diverse history and cultural influences. As a melting pot of civilizations, Malta's language has evolved to encompass a unique blend of linguistic elements, making it a fascinating subject of exploration and celebration.

At the core of Maltese identity is the Maltese language, Il-Lingwa Maltija, which holds the distinction of being the only Semitic language in the European Union. Rooted in the ancient language of the Phoenicians, Maltese has evolved over centuries, incorporating elements from Arabic, Italian, and English, among others. This linguistic fusion is a testament to Malta's history as a strategic crossroads for trade, culture, and conquest, where each civilization that left its mark contributed to the development of the island's vernacular.

The Arabic influence on Maltese is particularly pronounced, with over 40% of the language derived from this ancient tongue. This influence can be traced back to the Arab rule of the island in the 9th century, during which Arabic became the dominant language of administration and daily life. Today, many Maltese words and phrases bear the unmistakable imprint of Arabic, contributing to the island's linguistic charm. The Italian influence on Maltese language and culture is also significant, given Malta's proximity to Italy and the historical connections between the two regions. Italian loanwords and expressions have seamlessly integrated into Maltese speech, adding a touch of melodiousness and lyrical flair to everyday conversations. The Maltese language's ability to assimilate and adapt is evident in the way it continues to evolve, embracing modernity while preserving its traditional roots.

English holds a prominent position in Malta as the second official language, introduced during British colonial rule, which lasted from 1800 to 1964. The British influence on Malta's linguistic landscape is evident in its legal, administrative, and educational systems, all of which continue to function in English alongside Maltese. English proficiency is widespread across the island, making it a favored destination for English language learners and international students seeking quality education.

The unique bilingualism of Malta has not only fostered cross-cultural communication but has also facilitated the island's integration into the global community. English serves as a bridge between Malta and the world, opening doors for international trade, diplomacy, and tourism. Its widespread use has also attracted a diverse range of expatriates and international professionals who have chosen to make Malta their home, further enriching the island's multicultural fabric.

Beyond Maltese and English, Malta's linguistic landscape is also colored by a variety of other influences. The legacy of the Knights of St. John, a prominent military and religious order that ruled Malta during the 16th and 18th centuries, is evident in the presence of Latin in religious ceremonies and inscriptions. Additionally, Malta's contact with various European languages, including French and Spanish, has left subtle imprints on the island's linguistic repertoire.

Ancient Temples and Megalithic Structures - Malta's Prehistoric Heritage

In the sun-kissed embrace of the Mediterranean Sea lies Malta, an island steeped in the mystique of its prehistoric past. Malta's ancient temples and megalithic structures stand as enduring monuments to the ingenuity and spiritual fervor of its early inhabitants, a heritage that celebrates the island's profound connection to its distant past.

Dating back over 5,000 years, Malta's prehistoric temples are a testament to the advanced architectural skills and engineering prowess of its ancient builders. The Ġgantija temples on the island of Gozo, believed to be one of the oldest freestanding stone structures in the world, showcase colossal megaliths that defy the imagination. These temples were constructed during the Neolithic period, a time when the rest of Europe was still living in primitive settlements, making Malta a cradle of civilization far ahead of its time.

The Ħaġar Qim and Mnajdra temples, also UNESCO World Heritage Sites, are awe-inspiring examples of Malta's prehistoric architectural achievements. Perched on the cliffs overlooking the Mediterranean, these temples offer a breathtaking panorama and an opportunity to witness the harmony between ancient civilizations and the natural landscape. The precision of their construction and alignment with astronomical events is a testament to the deep spiritual beliefs and astronomical knowledge of Malta's prehistoric people.

The Hypogeum of Ħal-Saflieni is another remarkable prehistoric structure, a subterranean necropolis hewn out of the living rock. This underground complex of chambers and passages, intricately adorned with carvings and paintings, provides a haunting glimpse into the burial practices and beliefs of the ancient Maltese society. The preservation of the Hypogeum and its artistic features is a testament to the island's commitment to safeguarding its prehistoric heritage for future generations.

One of the most intriguing aspects of Malta's megalithic structures is the mystery surrounding their construction. The massive stone blocks used in their creation were transported over long distances without the aid of modern machinery, an engineering feat that remains the subject of ongoing research and speculation. The precision of their placement and the astronomical alignments in some temples suggest a sophisticated knowledge of architecture, astronomy, and mathematics among the ancient Maltese.

The significance of Malta's prehistoric temples extends beyond mere architectural marvels. These ancient structures provide a glimpse into the spiritual and cultural beliefs of the island's early inhabitants. Many of the temples are adorned with intricate carvings and statues, depicting fertility goddesses, animals, and spirals, offering clues to the spiritual practices and rituals of the ancient Maltese people.

The worship of the Great Mother Goddess, a central figure in many prehistoric societies, is evident in the figurines and artifacts found at the temples. This veneration of the feminine divine underscores the ancient Maltese society's deep connection to nature and the cycles of life, a theme that resonates throughout Malta's prehistoric heritage.

In addition to their spiritual significance, Malta's megalithic structures have also garnered attention for their astronomical alignments. Some temples are oriented to mark significant solar and lunar events, such as the solstices and equinoxes, demonstrating the advanced knowledge of astronomy possessed by the ancient Maltese people. These celestial alignments likely played a vital role in the religious and agricultural calendars, adding another layer of complexity to the temples' multifaceted significance.

The Knights of St. John - Malta's Medieval Legacy

In the annals of history, the Knights of St. John stand as a formidable force, and their presence in Malta has left an indelible mark on the island's cultural and architectural heritage. Originally known as the Knights Hospitaller, this chivalric order emerged during the 11th century with a noble mission to care for the sick and pilgrims in the Holy Land. Over time, their valor and devotion to their cause elevated them to a position of prominence and influence throughout Europe and the Mediterranean.

The Crusades of the Middle Ages were a defining era for the Knights of St. John, as they engaged in fierce battles to defend Christendom and safeguard the pilgrimage routes to Jerusalem. The Order's commitment to their mission earned them widespread respect, and their reputation for valor and benevolence spread far beyond their original mission of providing medical care.

As the Crusader states in the Holy Land faced decline, the Knights Hospitaller sought a new base of operations, leading to their establishment in Rhodes in 1310. Here, they fortified their position and expanded their military might, earning the epithet "Knights of Rhodes." Their stronghold on the island enabled them to protect Christian territories and repel invasions by Ottoman forces, earning the respect and admiration of European leaders and their subjects.

In 1530, Charles V of Spain bestowed the island of Malta upon the Knights of St. John as a fiefdom in recognition of their unwavering dedication and valor. This marked a pivotal moment in the history of Malta, as it set the stage for the Knights to forge their medieval legacy on the island.

Upon their arrival in Malta, the Knights embarked on an ambitious project to fortify the island, transforming it into an impregnable fortress against Ottoman advances. Their military prowess and expertise in fortifications were showcased in the construction of the awe-inspiring walls and bastions that still grace the island's landscape today. These formidable defenses played a crucial role in thwarting the Great Siege of Malta in 1565, a pivotal event that saw the Knights valiantly defend the island against overwhelming odds.

The Order's influence extended beyond military endeavors, as they engaged in charitable works and philanthropy to uplift the local population. The Knights established hospitals and schools, providing essential services and educational opportunities to the Maltese people. Their commitment to the welfare of the island's inhabitants earned them admiration and loyalty from the locals, further solidifying their place in Malta's history.

Malta's medieval legacy under the Knights of St. John is also manifested in the architectural wonders that grace the island. Magnificent palaces, churches, and auberges (inns) were constructed during their rule, showcasing their penchant for ornate design and opulence. The Grand Master's Palace, St. John's Co-Cathedral, and the auberges that housed the various langues (tongues) of the Order, stand as majestic edifices that pay tribute to the Knights' grandeur.

The influence of the Knights of St. John on Malta's culture extended to the arts as well. The Order fostered the development of the Maltese language and literature, with the publication of books in Maltese serving as a key milestone in the promotion of the island's vernacular. Their patronage of the arts also contributed to the flourishing of music, painting, and sculpture on the island.

The Great Siege of Malta - Defiance and Heroism Against the Ottomans

In the annals of military history, one epic chapter stands out as a testament to the indomitable spirit and valor of the Maltese people - The Great Siege of Malta. This epic confrontation, which unfolded from May 18 to September 8, 1565, pitted the Knights of St. John and the brave inhabitants of Malta against the formidable might of the Ottoman Empire, led by the legendary commander Suleiman the Magnificent. The Siege marked a pivotal moment in Malta's history, showcasing a fierce defiance and unwavering heroism that secured the island's survival and left a lasting impact on its cultural and national identity.

At the heart of The Great Siege was the Knights Hospitaller, known as the Knights of St. John, who had made Malta their home after being granted the island by Charles V of Spain in 1530. These valiant defenders were an eclectic mix of noble knights, seasoned soldiers, and resolute warriors from across Europe, united by their steadfast dedication to Christianity and the protection of Christendom. Under the leadership of Grand Master Jean de Valette, they forged an unyielding bond with the Maltese people, as both groups shared a common purpose - to safeguard their beloved homeland from the impending Ottoman onslaught.

Suleiman the Magnificent, the formidable Sultan of the Ottoman Empire, set his sights on Malta with the intent of expanding his empire's dominion and vanquishing the Knights Hospitaller, whose resilience had long been a thorn in the side of the Ottoman Empire. The Ottoman armada, a vast fleet of warships and galleys numbering over 200, set sail to lay siege to Malta, their ranks swelling with battle-hardened soldiers eager to claim the island for their Sultan.

The Ottomans arrived in Malta on May 18, 1565, and immediately launched a ferocious assault on the island's formidable defenses. The Knights and Maltese inhabitants had prepared well for this invasion, fortifying their strongholds and entrenching themselves within the imposing fortresses of Birgu, Senglea, and Mdina. The Siege became a grueling test of endurance and valor, as the Ottomans relentlessly bombarded the island with cannon fire and launched numerous land assaults, intent on breaking the spirit of the defenders.

The sheer determination and valor displayed by the defenders during The Great Siege was nothing short of awe-inspiring. Despite being outnumbered and facing overwhelming odds, they displayed a fervent resolve to protect their homes, families, and faith. The Knights Hospitaller and the Maltese warriors repelled wave after wave of Ottoman attacks, pushing back the invaders time and again with steadfast courage and unwavering unity.

The Siege was a test of endurance, as both sides endured a grueling summer in the Mediterranean heat. The Knights and Maltese inhabitants endured harsh conditions and limited provisions, yet they refused to yield. The Grand Master himself led by example, always at the forefront of the defense, inspiring his men and embodying the spirit of unwavering resolve.

The pivotal moment of The Great Siege came on September 1, 1565, when the Ottomans launched their final, all-out assault on the fortified city of Birgu. This climactic battle, known as the Battle of St. Elmo, saw the Knights valiantly defend the fortress against insurmountable odds. The Knights, led by a brave contingent of Spanish soldiers, fought with a ferocity and determination that surprised even their adversaries. Though St. Elmo eventually fell after a heroic resistance, its defense came at a heavy cost for the Ottomans, delaying their overall progress and bolstering the morale of the defenders.

The arrival of a much-needed reinforcement fleet from Spain on September 7, 1565, bolstered the spirits of the besieged, further dashing the hopes of the Ottoman invaders. The combined force of the Knights, the Maltese warriors, and the Spanish reinforcements launched a decisive counterattack, forcing the Ottomans to retreat in defeat.

The Great Siege of Malta concluded on September 8, 1565, with the Ottoman fleet abandoning the siege and withdrawing from the island. The defenders had achieved a resounding victory, fending off one of the most formidable military forces of the time. The Siege proved to be a defining moment in Malta's history, elevating the island's status from a mere strategic outpost to a symbol of defiance and resilience in the face of adversity.

The bravery and heroism displayed by the Knights of St. John and the Maltese inhabitants during The Great Siege reverberated across Europe, earning them widespread admiration and acclaim. The Pope bestowed the title "The Most Catholic Island" upon Malta, recognizing the island's unwavering commitment to Christianity and its valiant defense against the Ottoman Empire.

The Great Siege of Malta left an indelible mark on the collective memory of the Maltese people, shaping their national identity and fostering a sense of pride in their ancestors' heroic accomplishments. The Siege became a symbol of Malta's resilience and determination, inspiring future generations to uphold the spirit of valor and unity that defined this momentous chapter in the island's history. The echoes of The Great Siege continue to resonate through the ages, serving as a reminder of the enduring legacy of defiance and heroism that defines Malta's medieval heritage.

Valletta - The Grand Capital City and Its Architectural Marvels

In the heart of the Mediterranean lies Valletta, the magnificent capital city of Malta, a place where history, culture, and architecture intertwine in a mesmerizing tapestry. Named after its illustrious founder, Grand Master Jean de Valette, Valletta stands as a living testament to the valor and resilience of the Knights of St. John who defended Malta against the Ottoman onslaught during the Great Siege of 1565. This architectural marvel, often referred to as "The Fortress City," bears witness to the island's enduring spirit and the indomitable legacy of its medieval past.

Valletta's creation was a labor of love and a testament to the vision of its illustrious founder. After the Great Siege, Grand Master Jean de Valette sought to build a city that would forever commemorate the triumph of the Knights and the Maltese people. The peninsula of Mount Sceberras was chosen as the ideal location for this grand endeavor, as its strategic elevation provided a natural vantage point to monitor and defend the surrounding waters.

The construction of Valletta commenced in 1566 under the supervision of the renowned military engineer Francesco Laparelli, who devised an innovative grid-like street plan that optimized defense and facilitated ease of movement within the city. Valletta's layout was designed with military precision, characterized by straight streets that intersected at right angles, allowing for unobstructed views and swift access to its fortified bastions.

The architectural splendor of Valletta is a fusion of various styles and influences that span the ages. Its distinctive limestone buildings exude a golden hue, earning it the moniker "The City of Golden Stones." The baroque architecture, a hallmark of the 17th and 18th centuries, prevails throughout Valletta, showcasing ornate facades, grandiose churches, and elegant palaces adorned with intricate carvings and sculptures.

St. John's Co-Cathedral is one of the crown jewels of Valletta's architectural treasures. Completed in 1577, this opulent baroque cathedral was designed by the renowned Maltese architect Girolamo Cassar, who left an indelible mark on the city's skyline. The cathedral's facade is adorned with statues, columns, and the iconic coat of arms of Grand Master Jean de Valette, a symbol of his legacy and the Knights' triumph during the Great Siege.

The Grand Master's Palace, now home to the Office of the President of Malta, is a regal testament to the power and prestige of the Knights Hospitaller. The palace, originally built as the residence of the Grand Master, features opulent state rooms, lavishly decorated halls, and a spectacular armory showcasing a vast collection of medieval weaponry and armor.

Valletta's fortifications are a marvel of military engineering, exemplifying the Knights' dedication to protecting their city. The city's impressive bastions, fortified walls, and watchtowers stand as a testament to their strategic foresight and unmatched prowess in fortifications. These defenses played a crucial role in the Great Siege and continue to serve as a reminder of Valletta's enduring strength.

In addition to its architectural wonders, Valletta's streets and squares are adorned with statues and monuments that commemorate significant events and historical figures. The Triton Fountain, located at the entrance to the city, is a majestic fountain featuring statues symbolizing Malta's maritime heritage. The Siege Bell Memorial, situated at Lower Barrakka Gardens, pays tribute to the fallen defenders of the Great Siege.

Valletta's cultural heritage extends beyond its architecture, as the city boasts a vibrant arts scene, museums, and galleries that showcase Malta's artistic and historical treasures. The National Museum of Archaeology, the National Museum of Fine Arts, and the Malta Experience are just a few of the cultural institutions that provide visitors with a captivating journey through Malta's rich past.

Mdina - The Silent City, A Journey Through Time

Perched majestically on a hilltop, away from the hustle and bustle of modern life, lies Mdina, the enchanting "Silent City" of Malta. Stepping into Mdina is like stepping into a time capsule, where history unfolds before your eyes, and the echoes of the past resonate through its narrow cobbled streets. This ancient walled city is a treasure trove of architectural marvels and storied past, inviting visitors on a captivating journey through time.

Mdina's origins can be traced back to ancient times, dating as far back as the Phoenician era. Its strategic location atop a hill offered unparalleled views of the surrounding countryside and the sea, making it an ideal defensive stronghold for various civilizations throughout history. The Phoenicians, Romans, Arabs, and Knights of St. John all left their mark on Mdina, shaping its character and contributing to the unique blend of architectural styles that grace the city.

The name "Mdina" is derived from the Arabic word "medina," meaning "walled city," a testament to its fortified nature. The city's imposing bastions and sturdy walls stand as a testament to its historical significance and the need for protection during times of conflict. The panoramic views from the bastions offer breathtaking vistas of the Maltese landscape, providing a glimpse into the city's strategic importance throughout the ages.

As you wander through Mdina's silent streets, you'll be immersed in the timeless beauty of its architecture. The palaces, churches, and private residences showcase a stunning fusion of medieval, baroque, and neoclassical styles, reflecting the city's diverse history and cultural influences. The medieval architecture is particularly striking, with intricate stone facades, graceful archways, and finely wrought balconies, all adding to the city's ethereal charm.

One of Mdina's most iconic landmarks is the St. Paul's Cathedral, a striking baroque masterpiece that stands as a testament to the city's religious heritage. Originally built in the 12th century, the cathedral was extensively remodeled after the devastating earthquake of 1693. Its ornate interior is adorned with intricate sculptures, gilded altars, and magnificent paintings, a testimony to the city's devoutness and reverence.

Mdina is not only a city of stone and history but also a city of culture and art. Throughout its storied past, it has been a center of intellectual and artistic pursuits, attracting poets, writers, and musicians who sought inspiration within its silent walls. The city's timeless appeal has served as a backdrop for various films and television productions, further cementing its place in the hearts of artists and audiences alike.

The winding streets of Mdina offer surprises at every turn, with quaint alleys leading to charming squares, where locals gather and visitors soak in the tranquil atmosphere. Each street bears the weight of history, and each doorway conceals stories of generations past. The city's architectural heritage is carefully preserved, with strict regulations in place to protect its unique character and ensure that its charm endures for generations to come.

Exploring the Coastal Beauty - Maltese Beaches and Seaside Escapes

Beyond its rich history and cultural heritage, Malta beckons visitors with its breathtaking coastal beauty, a testament to the island's magnetic allure as a sun-soaked Mediterranean paradise. With its crystal-clear waters, golden sandy shores, and rugged cliffs, Malta boasts a diverse array of beaches and seaside escapes that cater to every traveler's delight.

Glimpses of the stunning Maltese coastline can be found in every corner of the island. From the picturesque coves of Comino to the hidden gems of Gozo and the bustling beaches of Malta, each seaside spot offers a unique and unforgettable experience. Whether you seek tranquility and seclusion or vibrant beachfront activities, Malta has it all.

For those yearning for secluded serenity, the Blue Lagoon in Comino is a must-visit destination. Accessible only by boat, this natural lagoon is a breathtaking oasis of turquoise waters and pristine white sands. Snorkeling in the Blue Lagoon's crystal-clear waters reveals a colorful underwater world, where vibrant marine life dances beneath the surface.

Gozo, Malta's sister island, is a treasure trove of hidden coastal gems. The red sands of Ramla Bay, backed by verdant hills and ancient ruins, provide a striking contrast to the deep blue sea. San Blas Bay, tucked away in a remote corner of Gozo, rewards intrepid travelers with its unspoiled beauty and sense of seclusion.

Back on the main island of Malta, Golden Bay and Ghajn Tuffieha offer two of the most celebrated beaches on the island. Golden Bay, with its expansive sandy shore, beckons visitors to unwind under the warm Mediterranean sun. Ghajn Tuffieha, accessible via a scenic staircase descending from the cliffs, rewards those who make the journey with stunning panoramic views and a secluded, untouched ambiance.

The coastline of Malta is dotted with quaint fishing villages that offer a glimpse into traditional island life. Marsaxlokk, famous for its Sunday fish market, is a charming spot to savor freshly caught seafood while admiring the colorful traditional fishing boats called "luzzus." The coastal village of Marsaskala boasts a long promenade and small sandy stretches, where locals and visitors come together to enjoy the sea breeze.

Adventure seekers and water sports enthusiasts will find their paradise on Malta's northeastern coast in Mellieha. This coastal hub is a hotspot for water-based activities, from kayaking and paddleboarding to jet skiing and windsurfing. Mellieha's Ghadira Bay, the largest sandy beach on the island, offers ample space to soak up the sun and engage in beachside fun.

Malta's coastline also presents a mesmerizing array of natural wonders, with its rugged cliffs and sea caves adding a sense of wild beauty to the island's shores. The Dingli Cliffs, towering over 200 meters above sea level, offer breathtaking views of the Mediterranean expanse, providing the perfect backdrop for a scenic coastal walk.

The Three Cities - A Glimpse into Malta's Maritime Past

Nestled on the southeastern coast of Malta, the Three Cities - Vittoriosa, Senglea, and Cospicua - beckon travelers on a captivating journey into the island's maritime past. These historic gems stand as living testaments to Malta's strategic importance in the Mediterranean and the indomitable spirit of its people throughout the ages. With their cobbled streets, ancient fortifications, and rich cultural heritage, the Three Cities offer a glimpse into a bygone era of seafaring glory and timeless charm.

Each of the Three Cities boasts a storied history, with origins dating back to ancient times. Vittoriosa, also known as Birgu, is the oldest of the three and served as the original home of the Knights of St. John upon their arrival in Malta in 1530. Its strategic location within the Grand Harbor made it an ideal base for the Knights to protect the island from potential invasions.

Senglea, also called Isla, sits on a narrow peninsula, flanked by two grand harbors, providing an unrivaled vantage point for observing maritime activity. Its fortifications were reinforced during the Great Siege of 1565, as the city played a crucial role in defending Malta from the Ottoman forces.

Cospicua, or Bormla, is the largest of the Three Cities and served as a center for maritime activities, with its shipyards and docks contributing to Malta's reputation as a naval power. The city's name, Cospicua, translates to "bountiful" in Italian, a nod to its historical significance as a flourishing maritime hub.

Throughout their histories, the Three Cities experienced waves of triumph and turmoil, with foreign powers vying for control of Malta's strategic harbors. The Knights of St. John's rule brought prosperity and fortification, transforming the cities into formidable bastions of defense. However, they also faced challenges, including the brief occupation by Napoleon Bonaparte's forces in 1798.

One of the defining moments in the Three Cities' history was the pivotal role they played during the Great Siege of 1565. The Knights and the Maltese people's heroic defense of Vittoriosa, Senglea, and Cospicua against the invading Ottoman forces under Suleiman the Magnificent earned them widespread acclaim and solidified their reputation as guardians of the Mediterranean.

The architectural heritage of the Three Cities is a reflection of their illustrious past. Each city is adorned with elegant palaces, stately churches, and grand fortifications that narrate the stories of the past. The Inquisitor's Palace in Vittoriosa stands as a remarkable example of Baroque architecture, providing a glimpse into the opulent lifestyle of the Inquisitor during the Knights' rule.

The fortifications of the Three Cities remain a testament to their strategic significance. The massive defensive walls, fortified bastions, and watchtowers that encircle the cities are a reminder of their military prowess and their determination to protect Malta from external threats.

Stepping into the Three Cities is akin to stepping back in time, where every stone and facade holds tales of courage, valor, and maritime adventures. The narrow streets, evocative of an era long past, are alive with the echoes of history, inviting visitors to immerse themselves in the bygone world of sailors, merchants, and knights.

Today, the Three Cities are vibrant cultural hubs, blending the richness of their maritime past with modern life. Visitors can stroll through the charming streets, visit museums, and explore the fascinating history of the cities. The waterfront promenades offer picturesque views of the Grand Harbor, where traditional Maltese boats known as "dghajsa" glide gracefully across the water.

Gozo and Comino - The Enchanting Sister Islands

Beyond the shores of Malta lie two enchanting sister islands - Gozo and Comino, each with its own distinct charm and allure, adding to the magical tapestry of the Maltese archipelago. These gems of the Mediterranean invite travelers to escape to a world of serenity, natural beauty, and authentic island life.

Gozo, the second-largest island of the Maltese archipelago, is a haven of tranquility and rural charm. Fondly referred to as "The Island of Calypso," Gozo is steeped in legend, with ancient myth linking it to Homer's epic Odyssey. Its pristine landscapes, dotted with fertile valleys, quaint villages, and limestone hills, create a postcard-worthy setting that captivates the soul.

Gozo's heart lies in its picturesque villages, where time seems to slow down, and the traditions of old continue to thrive. Victoria, the capital city, is a bustling hub with a rich history that dates back to the medieval era. Its imposing citadel, perched atop a hill, offers panoramic views of the island and serves as a reminder of Gozo's strategic significance throughout the ages.

The countryside of Gozo is adorned with charming farmhouses and traditional rural architecture, evoking a sense of nostalgia for simpler times. The Citadel's surroundings are scattered with ancient churches and basilicas, many of which boast awe-inspiring baroque architecture and intricate artworks, reflecting the island's deep-rooted religious traditions.

The coastline of Gozo offers a treasure trove of natural wonders, where azure waters embrace secluded coves and rocky cliffs. Ramla Bay, with its reddish-golden sands and crystal-clear waters, stands as a favorite among both locals and visitors. Dwejra, a former coastal inlet now transformed into a breathtaking geological site, once housed the iconic Azure Window, a limestone arch that became a symbol of Gozo's unique beauty.

Comino, the smallest of the Maltese islands, is a captivating slice of paradise known for its unspoiled landscapes and azure-blue waters. Measuring just 3.5 square kilometers, Comino's appeal lies in its pristine nature and peaceful ambiance, offering a serene escape from the world's hustle and bustle.

Comino is a car-free island, allowing visitors to explore its natural wonders on foot or by bicycle. The island's main attraction, the Blue Lagoon, is a mesmerizing haven of turquoise waters and chalk-white sands, attracting boaters and snorkelers alike. The lagoon's crystalline waters teem with marine life, offering an underwater paradise to explore.

Beyond the Blue Lagoon, Comino's rugged coastline hides many secret coves and sea caves, making it a haven for adventurers seeking to discover hidden gems. Santa Marija Bay and San Niklaw Bay are two such spots, offering an idyllic setting to bask in the Mediterranean sun and enjoy the soothing sound of the sea.

Throughout the year, Gozo and Comino come alive with vibrant festivities that celebrate their cultural heritage and religious traditions. The village feasts, known as "festas," are a beloved tradition, with each village honoring its patron saint through processions, fireworks, and communal gatherings that unite locals and visitors in joyous celebration.

Gozo and Comino also embrace a rich culinary heritage, with locally sourced ingredients and traditional recipes passed down through generations. The islands' gastronomic offerings include delectable seafood dishes, freshly harvested produce, and artisanal cheeses, providing a tantalizing journey for the taste buds.

The charm of Gozo and Comino lies not only in their picturesque landscapes but also in the warmth and hospitality of their people. The genuine smiles and friendly greetings from locals exude a sense of welcoming, making visitors feel like they have discovered a second home.

Gozo and Comino, the enchanting sister islands, continue to captivate the hearts of travelers from around the world. They offer an escape from the ordinary and an invitation to embrace the simple joys of life. Whether exploring Gozo's rustic countryside or immersing oneself in Comino's serene coastal beauty, these islands hold an irresistible allure that celebrates the essence of Malta - a captivating blend of history, culture, and natural splendor.

Malta's Art and Artists - A Canvas of Creativity

In the heart of the Mediterranean, Malta's artistic spirit weaves a vibrant tapestry of creativity, drawing inspiration from its rich history, diverse cultural influences, and breathtaking landscapes. Throughout the ages, the island has nurtured a community of talented artists who have left an indelible mark on the world of art, showcasing their unique perspectives through various mediums.

The roots of Maltese art can be traced back to prehistoric times, evident in the ancient megalithic temples that bear intricate carvings and artistic expressions. These prehistoric artifacts, such as the awe-inspiring Hal Saflieni Hypogeum, provide a glimpse into the island's artistic heritage, highlighting the enduring creative spirit of its ancient inhabitants.

The influence of the various civilizations that have left their mark on Malta is also evident in its art. The Phoenicians, Romans, Arabs, and Knights of St. John all contributed to the island's cultural landscape, enriching its artistic traditions and inspiring local artists to draw from a diverse palette of influences.

One of the defining moments in Maltese art history was the arrival of the Knights of St. John in the 16th century. The Knights' patronage of the arts and their influence from the Italian Renaissance brought about a flourishing period of artistic expression. Lavish churches, ornate palaces, and exquisite sculptures adorned the island, reflecting the grandeur and opulence of the era.

The baroque period that followed saw the emergence of prolific Maltese artists who left an indelible mark on the art world. The renowned painter Mattia Preti, known as "Il Cavalier Calabrese," was one such luminary who graced Malta with his exceptional talent. His masterpieces can still be admired in the St. John's Co-Cathedral, where his ceiling paintings depict scenes from the life of St. John the Baptist.

As the world evolved, so did Maltese art. The 20th century brought forth a wave of modernism, with local artists embracing new techniques and styles, while continuing to draw inspiration from the island's rich heritage. Maltese artists explored various mediums, from painting and sculpture to photography, ceramics, and digital art, creating a diverse and dynamic art scene that continues to evolve.

Gozo, Malta's sister island, has also been a nurturing ground for artistic expression. The island's serene landscapes, charming villages, and sense of tranquility have inspired artists to capture its essence on canvas and through other creative outlets. The rugged cliffs, quaint alleys, and picturesque countryside serve as a muse for many local artists, infusing their works with the spirit of Gozo.

Today, Malta's art scene continues to thrive, with numerous galleries, exhibitions, and art festivals celebrating the creativity of local and international artists. The Valletta International Arts Festival, held annually, brings together artists from various disciplines to showcase their talents and foster cultural exchange.

In addition to traditional art forms, street art has also gained prominence in Malta, with colorful murals adorning the walls of urban spaces, breathing new life into the cityscape. These vibrant works of art add a contemporary twist to the island's artistic heritage, offering a visual feast to locals and visitors alike.

Malta's artists, both past, and present, continue to inspire and be inspired by the island's timeless beauty. From capturing the play of light on its limestone facades to immortalizing the Mediterranean's azure hues, they celebrate the essence of Malta through their artistic expressions.

The Maltese Carnival - Revelry and Merriment

Amidst the ancient stone walls and historic streets of Malta, a vibrant celebration comes to life each year during the Maltese Carnival, a joyous occasion that unites the island in revelry and merriment. Rooted in centuries-old traditions, the Carnival stands as a testament to Malta's cultural heritage and the indomitable spirit of its people.

The origins of the Maltese Carnival can be traced back to the medieval era, where it was celebrated as a prelude to the forty-day period of Lent, leading up to Easter. The word "Carnival" itself is derived from the Latin phrase "carne vale," meaning "farewell to meat," as the festive occasion marks the final indulgence in rich foods and merry-making before the period of fasting and reflection.

Each year, the streets of Malta come alive with a riot of colors, music, and elaborate costumes during the Carnival. Festivities kick off with the grand opening parade, known as "il-karnival ta' Malta," where locals and visitors alike gather to witness a spectacle of floats, dancers, and musicians moving through the streets of Valletta, Malta's capital city.

The Carnival is characterized by an array of distinctive and often humorous masks and costumes. The traditional "kukkanja" is a towering headdress adorned with mirrors, feathers, and colorful fabrics, worn by participants to conceal their identity and immerse themselves in the spirit of celebration. Additionally, "kukkanji," clad in outlandish outfits, entertain the crowd with lively performances and witty jests.

Throughout the Carnival, "defile" or costume competitions are held, where participants showcase their meticulously crafted ensembles, vying for recognition and accolades for their creativity and artistry. The costumes range from traditional historical figures to modern pop culture icons, demonstrating the Carnival's ability to blend tradition with contemporary influences.

Music plays a central role in the festivities, with vibrant brass bands, drummers, and musicians filling the air with infectious rhythms and melodies. The sound of laughter and dancing feet echoes through the streets as the Carnival spirit takes hold of the island.

The Carnival celebrations extend to various towns and villages across Malta and Gozo, each adding its own unique flair and traditions. Nadur, a village in Gozo, is particularly renowned for its spontaneous and lively Carnival revelries, known as "il-karnival ta' Ghawdex." The Nadur Carnival embraces a more satirical and irreverent approach, often poking fun at political figures and societal norms through its witty and comedic performances.

During the Carnival, the Maltese people and visitors of all ages come together, transcending social divides and cultural backgrounds, to partake in the festivities. The spirit of camaraderie and unity is palpable, as the Carnival serves as a time for families, friends, and strangers to bond and share in the joyous celebration.

One of the most anticipated events during the Carnival is the "bragazzi," a colorful parade of children dressed in costumes, parading through the streets with youthful exuberance and innocence. This tradition fosters a sense of pride and excitement among the young participants, as they experience the joy of the Carnival firsthand.

As the final day of the Carnival approaches, the celebrations reach a crescendo with the "il-quċċija" or burial of the Carnival. Symbolizing the end of the revelry, a symbolic figure representing the Carnival is laid to rest, marking the transition to the somber and reflective period of Lent.

The Maltese Carnival, with its vibrant pageantry and joyous spirit, serves as a testament to Malta's cultural resilience and enduring traditions. It is a time for the island to come together, celebrate its heritage, and embrace the joy of life. The Carnival stands as a vivid expression of the Maltese people's ability to find happiness and camaraderie in the face of challenges, making it a cherished celebration that leaves an everlasting impression on the hearts of all who experience its revelry and merriment.

Music and Dance - The Rhythms of Malta's Soul

In the heart of the Mediterranean, the rhythms of music and dance resonate with the soul of Malta, weaving a captivating tapestry of cultural expression that reflects the island's rich history and vibrant spirit. For centuries, music and dance have played a central role in the lives of the Maltese people, serving as a medium through which they celebrate, mourn, and forge bonds that transcend time.

Traditional Maltese music is deeply rooted in the island's folklore and historical events. Folk songs, known as "ghana," are an essential part of Malta's musical heritage, recounting tales of love, bravery, and the struggles of everyday life. Passed down through generations, these songs are performed in a unique style known as "cantilena," characterized by melodic ornamentations and expressive vocal techniques.

The traditional Maltese folk ensemble, known as "ghana," features a blend of instruments, such as the guitar, mandolin, accordion, and traditional percussion instruments like the tambourine and the "żaqq." The distinct sound of the Maltese ghana ensemble captures the essence of the island's rustic charm, evoking a sense of nostalgia for simpler times.

Malta's music also reflects the island's religious devotion and the profound influence of the Catholic Church. Choral singing has a significant presence in Maltese culture, with many villages and towns boasting their own local choirs. The most notable of these choral traditions is the "Mudajjal" singing style, characterized by its rhythmic and harmonic complexity, performed during religious festivities and processions.

In addition to its traditional music, Malta has embraced various musical genres from around the world, infusing the island's musical landscape with a cosmopolitan flair. Pop, rock, jazz, and classical music have all found their place on the Maltese stage, with local artists garnering recognition both locally and internationally.

One of the most beloved musical events in Malta is the "Malta International Jazz Festival," where jazz enthusiasts from around the world gather to enjoy performances by acclaimed artists in the enchanting setting of Valletta's Grand Harbor.

Dance is an integral part of Malta's cultural identity, serving as a celebration of life and a reflection of its diverse heritage. The "Festa," a traditional village feast dedicated to a patron saint, is an occasion where lively and colorful folk dances are performed, showcasing the island's communal spirit and sense of community.

The "Għana" music, with its distinct rhythms and infectious melodies, provides the soundtrack for traditional Maltese folk dances. The "Għannejja," the traditional Maltese dancers, sway and twirl to the beat, telling stories through their graceful movements, evoking a sense of unity and celebration.

In addition to its traditional folk dances, Malta has embraced various modern dance styles, including contemporary, hip-hop, and ballroom. Dance schools and academies across the island offer training and opportunities for both aspiring and seasoned dancers to showcase their talents.

The performing arts are celebrated in Malta through numerous festivals and events that showcase the island's rich musical and dance traditions. The "Notte Bianca" or White Night festival, held annually in Valletta, is a vibrant celebration of arts and culture, where the streets come alive with performances, exhibitions, and music concerts, drawing locals and visitors alike.

The Malta Philharmonic Orchestra, established in 1968, stands as a beacon of musical excellence, delighting audiences with its performances of classical masterpieces and contemporary compositions. The orchestra collaborates with international musicians and conductors, further enriching the island's musical landscape.

Music and dance in Malta are more than just forms of entertainment; they are a reflection of the island's soul and its enduring spirit. The rhythms and melodies that emanate from the hearts of the Maltese people celebrate their unique heritage and their ability to embrace cultural diversity while preserving their cherished traditions.

Whether it's the stirring sounds of the "ghana" songs or the captivating movements of traditional folk dances, music and dance in Malta are a celebration of life, a testament to the island's resilience, and a timeless expression of joy that resonates with all who experience the rhythms of Malta's soul.

The Maltese Handicrafts - Preserving Traditional Artistry

In the sun-kissed corners of Malta, a world of exquisite craftsmanship unfolds, where the hands of skilled artisans breathe life into timeless traditions and preserve the island's rich cultural heritage. The Maltese handicrafts stand as a testament to the island's deep-rooted artisanal spirit and its commitment to safeguarding the artistry of yesteryears for generations to come.

Throughout the ages, Maltese handicrafts have been an integral part of the island's cultural fabric, with each craft carrying a story of heritage and artistic ingenuity. Passed down from master to apprentice, these traditional skills have survived the test of time, weaving a tapestry of artistic expression that mirrors the soul of Malta.

One of the most celebrated Maltese handicrafts is "filigree" jewelry, an intricate art form that dates back to the Phoenician era. Skilled artisans craft delicate jewelry pieces using fine silver or gold wires, intricately twisted and soldered together to form exquisite patterns and designs. Filigree jewelry showcases the precision and attention to detail of the Maltese artisans, making it a cherished and timeless keepsake for both locals and visitors.

Another revered craft is "ganutell," the art of creating intricate handmade flowers using wire and thread. Ganutell flowers are often used to adorn religious statues, bridal bouquets, and decorative pieces, reflecting the island's devotion to religious traditions and its appreciation for beauty in simplicity.

The craft of "qubbajt" or nougat-making is deeply ingrained in Maltese culture, especially during festive occasions like Christmas and weddings. Artisans skillfully blend honey, nuts, and sugar, transforming them into delectable treats that delight the taste buds and evoke a sense of nostalgia for cherished family traditions.

Maltese pottery is another remarkable craft that has stood the test of time. From functional kitchenware to ornate decorative pieces, local potters mold clay into objects of artistry, often featuring traditional designs and motifs inspired by Malta's landscapes and folklore.

The art of lace-making, known as "bizzilla," holds a special place in Maltese handicrafts. Intricate lace patterns are carefully hand-stitched using fine threads, and the finished pieces are cherished as heirlooms, passed down through generations as symbols of love and heritage.

The Maltese "karta lantin," or silverware, showcases the skill of silversmiths who create beautiful and ornate objects, ranging from candlesticks and trays to religious artifacts. The "ċwiegel," or traditional Maltese balconies, often feature decorative ironwork, a testament to the craftsmanship of local blacksmiths who skillfully forge intricate designs.

Malta's traditional wooden balconies, known as "gallarija," also exemplify the island's dedication to preserving architectural heritage. Carpenters meticulously carve and craft these stunning wooden structures, which adorn buildings throughout the island, adding a touch of elegance and authenticity to the urban landscape.

Throughout the year, Malta hosts various craft fairs and exhibitions, providing a platform for local artisans to showcase their creations and connect with art enthusiasts from around the world. These events celebrate the diversity of Maltese handicrafts and serve as a testament to the island's commitment to preserving its artistic heritage.

The Maltese government, alongside various cultural organizations, plays a crucial role in supporting and promoting traditional handicrafts. Workshops and training programs are organized to ensure that these time-honored skills are passed down to future generations, safeguarding the continuity of Malta's artisanal legacy.

The Maltese handicrafts are not merely objects of beauty; they embody the essence of Malta's cultural identity and its enduring commitment to honoring its past. As artisans lovingly shape each piece, they carry the stories of generations, infusing every creation with the spirit of their ancestors.

In a world where mass-produced goods dominate, the artistry of Maltese handicrafts stands as a beacon of authenticity and an ode to the enduring value of traditional craftsmanship. These handmade treasures serve as a testament to Malta's pride in its cultural heritage and its dedication to preserving the artistry that defines the island's soul, making the Maltese handicrafts a cherished and irreplaceable aspect of the island's identity.

Religious Festivals and Pilgrimages - A Profound Spiritual Experience

Amidst the picturesque landscapes and historical charm of Malta, religious festivals and pilgrimages stand as a profound expression of the island's unwavering faith and deep-rooted religious traditions. Malta, with its rich history as a stronghold of Catholicism, offers a plethora of spiritual experiences that resonate with the devout and captivate the hearts of visitors from all walks of life.

The Maltese people's religious fervor is palpable throughout the year, with a calendar brimming with religious feasts and observances that bring the community together in celebration and devotion. Each village, town, and city takes pride in honoring its patron saint with exuberant processions, elaborate decorations, and heartfelt prayers.

The feast of St. Paul's Shipwreck, celebrated on February 10th, stands as a prominent religious event on the island. It commemorates the shipwreck of St. Paul on the shores of Malta, as recounted in the Bible's Acts of the Apostles. The feast's grandeur is exemplified by the procession of St. Paul's statue through the streets of Valletta, accompanied by a sea of faithful followers and the thunderous sounds of brass bands.

Another significant feast is that of Our Lady of Mount Carmel, celebrated on July 16th. The procession of the statue of the Blessed Virgin Mary in Valletta is a sight to behold, as the faithful gather to pay homage and seek blessings from the patroness of Malta.

The feast of the Assumption of Mary, observed on August 15th, is a national public holiday and a time of great celebration. The feast pays homage to the belief that the Virgin Mary was assumed into heaven after her earthly life. Processions, church services, and elaborate decorations adorn the towns and villages as the Maltese people honor the Blessed Virgin.

One of the most spectacular religious events in Malta is the Good Friday processions, which take place across the island. These solemn and poignant processions reenact the Passion of Christ, with statues and scenes depicting the final hours of Jesus' life carried through the streets as a profound expression of faith and devotion.

Lent, the period leading up to Easter, is a time of reflection and spiritual contemplation for the Maltese people. Churches hold special liturgical services, and many individuals observe fasting and abstinence as they prepare for the joyous celebration of Easter Sunday.

Pilgrimages hold a special place in the hearts of the Maltese people, who embark on journeys of faith to sacred sites both within Malta and beyond its shores. The Sanctuary of Our Lady of Mellieha, dedicated to the Blessed Virgin Mary, is a cherished pilgrimage site that attracts devotees seeking solace and blessings.

Another significant pilgrimage site is the Ta' Pinu Basilica in Gozo, where countless faithful seek the intercession of Our Lady of Ta' Pinu. The basilica's history is replete with stories of miraculous healings and answered prayers, enhancing its spiritual significance.

The island of Comino is home to the Chapel of St. Mary's Tower, which holds a special place in the hearts of seafarers who seek protection and guidance from the patroness of the sea. Many sailors and fishermen pay their respects and seek blessings before embarking on voyages.

Pilgrimages also extend beyond Malta's shores, with many Maltese people journeying to religious sites in Italy, Spain, and other European countries. The allure of these sacred places draws the faithful, who seek spiritual renewal and a deeper connection with their faith.

The Maltese people's dedication to religious festivals and pilgrimages reflects their profound and unwavering faith, transcending generations and embracing the island's diverse cultural heritage. These spiritual experiences not only bring the community together but also offer an opportunity for visitors to witness the authentic expressions of Malta's religious soul.

As the fervor of religious celebrations and pilgrimages continues to endure, Malta remains a place where spirituality and cultural heritage converge, enriching the lives of its people and welcoming visitors to partake in the profound spiritual experiences that have shaped the island's identity for centuries.

Malta's Diverse Architecture - From Baroque to Modernism

Malta's architectural landscape is a living testament to the island's rich history and cultural tapestry, where the vestiges of ancient civilizations coexist harmoniously with the innovations of modern design. From grand baroque masterpieces to contemporary structures, Malta's diverse architecture tells a compelling story of the island's enduring spirit and its ability to embrace change while honoring its past.

One of the most prominent architectural influences in Malta is the Baroque style, which flourished during the rule of the Knights of St. John in the 16th and 17th centuries. The Knights' patronage of the arts and architecture left an indelible mark on the island, with grand palaces, opulent churches, and imposing fortifications gracing the Maltese landscape.

Valletta, Malta's capital city and a UNESCO World Heritage Site, is a treasure trove of Baroque architecture. The city's impressive fortifications, designed by the renowned military engineer Francesco Laparelli, are a testament to the Knights' strategic prowess and their dedication to protecting the island from invasions.

The jewel of Valletta's Baroque architecture is undoubtedly St. John's Co-Cathedral. Designed by the Maltese architect Girolamo Cassar, the cathedral's unassuming façade conceals a breathtaking interior adorned with intricate marble, gilded stuccoes, and striking baroque artwork. Mattia Preti, the famed Calabrian artist, contributed his masterful paintings to the cathedral, making it a true gem of Baroque artistry.

Beyond Valletta, Malta's cities and villages are adorned with Baroque treasures, each reflecting the unique identity of its locality. Mdina, the ancient capital of Malta, boasts majestic palaces and imposing bastions that offer breathtaking panoramic views of the surrounding landscapes. The baroque splendor of Mdina's Vilhena Palace, which now houses the National Museum of Natural History, stands as a testament to the island's architectural heritage.

As the world evolved, so did Malta's architecture. The 19th and early 20th centuries saw a transition from Baroque to Neoclassical and Victorian architectural styles. The British colonial influence during this period introduced new design elements, as seen in the elegant facades and wrought iron balconies that embellish many buildings in Valletta and other towns.

In the early 20th century, Malta embraced Art Nouveau, a movement characterized by its organic and decorative motifs. The "Auberge de Castille," one of the grandest buildings in Valletta and the current office of the Prime Minister of Malta, exemplifies this architectural style with its elaborate details and graceful curves.

The 20th century brought forth the emergence of modernism in Malta, with architects experimenting with functionalist principles and minimalist aesthetics. The Malta Festival Hall, designed by Richard England, is an exemplary modernist structure that showcases the island's adaptation to contemporary architectural trends.

Post-independence, Malta witnessed a surge of modernist and brutalist architecture, reflecting the island's aspirations for progress and urban development. The Malta University Campus, designed by renowned architect Richard England, exemplifies brutalist architecture with its raw concrete surfaces and geometric forms.

Today, Malta's architectural landscape continues to evolve, embracing sustainable design principles and contemporary aesthetics. The cityscape of Sliema and St. Julian's features modern high-rise buildings, while projects like the City Gate and Parliament Building in Valletta, designed by architect Renzo Piano, are a testament to the island's commitment to modern architecture that coexists harmoniously with its historic surroundings.

Malta's diverse architecture is a testament to the island's resilience and its ability to adapt to changing times while preserving its cultural heritage. Whether it's the grand baroque palaces, the elegant Victorian facades, or the innovative modernist structures, each building in Malta weaves a unique narrative that celebrates the island's rich history and its progressive spirit. As Malta continues to evolve, its architecture serves as a tangible expression of the island's identity, leaving an indelible mark on the hearts of all who experience its diverse architectural wonders.

Exploring Malta's Underwater World - Scuba Diving and Marine Reserves

Beneath the shimmering surface of the Mediterranean lies a world of enchantment and wonder, where Malta's underwater treasures beckon explorers and adventure-seekers alike. The island's crystal-clear waters and thriving marine life make it a scuba diving paradise and a haven for those eager to delve into the depths of the sea.

Malta's unique geographical location, at the crossroads of ancient civilizations, has endowed its underwater landscape with a rich history and a plethora of shipwrecks waiting to be discovered. The clear visibility and calm waters make scuba diving in Malta a rewarding experience, revealing a window into the past as divers encounter submerged relics from ancient times to the present.

One of the most iconic and accessible shipwrecks for divers is the "MV Rozi." Sunk intentionally in 1992, this tugboat now rests upright on the seabed off the coast of Cirkewwa. The wreck has become an artificial reef teeming with marine life, attracting divers of all levels to explore its fascinating interior and observe the colorful array of fish that have made it their home.

The "HMS Maori," a World War II destroyer, is another popular dive site near Valletta. Resting in relatively shallow waters, the wreck provides a unique opportunity for divers to explore its gun turrets, anchors, and engine room, all while surrounded by shoals of fish that call the wreck home.

For more experienced divers seeking a challenge, the "Um El Faroud" offers an unforgettable experience. This former oil tanker, deliberately scuttled in 1998 off the coast of Wied iz-Zurrieq, is one of the largest wrecks in the Mediterranean. Its impressive size and depth, reaching over 30 meters, provide a fascinating exploration of its vast interior and an encounter with abundant marine life.

Beyond shipwrecks, Malta's underwater world boasts mesmerizing natural features, including stunning caves, dramatic rock formations, and vibrant reefs. The "Blue Hole" in Gozo, a spectacular vertical chimney leading into a stunning underwater cave, is a favorite among divers seeking a surreal diving experience. The "Cathedral Cave" and "Reqqa Point" are also renowned for their unique rock formations and diverse marine life.

Marine reserves and protected areas are crucial for conserving Malta's underwater biodiversity. The "Dwejra Marine Nature Reserve," located off the coast of Gozo, is a sanctuary for marine life, featuring submerged sea arches and caves that attract an abundance of fish and other sea creatures.

The "Malta National Aquarium" in Qawra offers a different perspective on Malta's underwater world, allowing visitors to observe marine life up close without diving into the sea. The aquarium's exhibits showcase the incredible variety of marine species found around the Maltese islands, emphasizing the importance of protecting these fragile ecosystems.

In recent years, Malta has shown a commitment to marine conservation and sustainable diving practices. Efforts to protect marine life include the establishment of no-take zones and the implementation of strict regulations to safeguard the underwater environment. These conservation measures are crucial for preserving Malta's marine biodiversity and ensuring future generations can continue to enjoy the wonders of the sea.

Diving schools and centers across Malta cater to divers of all levels, providing expert guidance and equipment to ensure safe and enjoyable underwater experiences. The warm and welcoming nature of the Maltese people extends to the diving community, making it an ideal destination for both novice and seasoned divers.

Beyond the allure of shipwrecks and marine life, scuba diving in Malta fosters a sense of connection with nature and an appreciation for the delicate balance of life beneath the waves. As divers submerge into the turquoise waters, they become part of a timeless dance of marine creatures and seascapes, celebrating Malta's underwater world and its awe-inspiring beauty that lies just beneath the surface.

Sustainable Tourism in Malta - Balancing Preservation and Development

Nestled in the heart of the Mediterranean, Malta beckons travelers with its timeless allure and captivating landscapes. As tourists from around the globe flock to this idyllic island, the delicate balance between preservation and development takes center stage in the quest for sustainable tourism.

Malta's rich history, cultural heritage, and stunning natural beauty make it a magnet for tourists seeking authentic experiences and a glimpse into the past. From the ancient temples of Ħaġar Qim and Mnajdra to the grandeur of Valletta's baroque architecture, Malta's treasures are a testament to the island's enduring spirit and its commitment to preserving its heritage.

One of Malta's most cherished cultural assets is the "Knights' Festival" held annually in Valletta. This vibrant celebration pays homage to the island's medieval past, attracting visitors with its reenactments, historical processions, and medieval marketplaces that transport them back in time.

Beyond its historical charm, Malta's natural wonders enthrall travelers with their pristine beauty. The Blue Lagoon on Comino Island, with its crystal-clear turquoise waters, is a popular destination for sun-seekers and snorkelers eager to explore its underwater marvels. The island's rugged coastlines, dramatic cliffs, and hidden coves provide an array of opportunities for eco-tourism and outdoor enthusiasts.

As Malta's popularity as a tourist destination grows, so does the need for responsible tourism practices that safeguard its environment and cultural heritage. Sustainable tourism in Malta is a concerted effort to protect the island's natural and cultural assets while providing visitors with authentic experiences that benefit the local community.

The Maltese government, along with various organizations and businesses, has taken significant steps to promote sustainable tourism. Measures have been implemented to protect sensitive ecosystems, such as the creation of marine reserves and no-take zones to conserve underwater biodiversity.

To reduce the environmental impact of tourism, Malta encourages eco-friendly transportation and the use of renewable energy sources. Bike-sharing initiatives and electric vehicle rentals have been introduced to promote cleaner transportation options for visitors.

Malta's commitment to sustainable tourism extends to its accommodation sector. Many hotels and resorts have adopted eco-friendly practices, such as water and energy conservation measures and waste recycling programs, to minimize their ecological footprint.

Community-based tourism initiatives have flourished, allowing travelers to immerse themselves in the local way of life and support small businesses and artisans. Tourists can participate in traditional Maltese cooking classes, learn about local crafts, and visit family-run farms to gain a deeper appreciation for the island's cultural heritage.

To ensure that the benefits of tourism reach all segments of society, Malta embraces inclusive tourism practices that cater to diverse needs. The island offers accessible attractions, facilities, and services for travelers with disabilities, making it an inclusive destination that celebrates diversity and welcomes all visitors.

Education and awareness play a crucial role in promoting sustainable tourism in Malta. Tour guides and tourism operators are encouraged to provide responsible tourism information to visitors, raising awareness about the importance of preserving the island's natural beauty and cultural heritage.

Through collaboration and shared responsibility, Malta continues to strike a balance between preserving its precious heritage and embracing responsible development. The island's commitment to sustainable tourism ensures that future generations can also experience the magic of Malta and the timeless connection between preservation and progress.

As travelers from around the world discover the beauty and allure of Malta, they become guardians of the island's heritage, embracing the responsibility to cherish and protect this Mediterranean gem. Sustainable tourism in Malta is a journey of celebration, an opportunity for travelers to forge a deep connection with the island, and an enduring commitment to preserving its splendor for generations to come.

The Maltese Countryside - Rural Traditions and Breathtaking Landscapes

Amidst the vibrant cultural hubs and historical landmarks of Malta lies a hidden gem, the enchanting Maltese countryside. Away from the bustling cities and crowded beaches, the rural landscapes of Malta offer a serene escape into a world of timeless traditions and breathtaking beauty.

The Maltese countryside is a patchwork of rolling hills, fertile valleys, and quaint villages that have stood the test of time. Here, the pace of life slows down, and the bond with nature runs deep. The terraced fields, meticulously crafted by generations of farmers, bear witness to the island's agricultural heritage and the resourcefulness of its people.

In the heart of the countryside, traditional farmhouses with their distinctive limestone facades stand as a testament to Malta's rural architecture. These charming structures, often adorned with colorful doors and windows, blend harmoniously with the natural surroundings, offering a glimpse into the simple and authentic way of life that defines rural Malta.

The rhythm of the countryside is governed by the seasons, and each time of the year brings its own palette of colors and experiences. Spring blankets the landscapes with vibrant wildflowers and blossoming almond trees, creating a picturesque setting that has inspired artists and poets alike.

Summer, with its golden sun and azure skies, brings the Maltese countryside to life with the buzzing of insects and the chirping of birds. As the sun sets over the fields, a symphony of crickets and frogs fills the air, creating an enchanting ambiance that feels like a timeless lullaby.

Autumn is a time of harvest and celebration, as farmers reap the fruits of their labor, and villages come together for traditional feasts and festivals. The air is filled with the aroma of freshly harvested grapes and the scent of fig trees, a sensory delight that resonates with the soul.

Winter casts a different spell on the Maltese countryside, painting the fields with lush greenery and rejuvenating the land. While the chill in the air brings a sense of coziness, it also heralds the arrival of the festive season, when rural traditions and customs are passed down through generations.

The Maltese countryside is more than just picturesque landscapes; it is a treasure trove of rural traditions that have shaped the island's identity. Agricultural practices, such as olive and wine production, have been handed down through centuries, preserving the knowledge and skills of previous generations.

Villages in the countryside are the heart of community life, where local traditions and festivities thrive. Religious feasts, village fairs, and folklore events bring the community together, fostering a sense of unity and belonging that echoes through the ages.

The rural landscapes of Malta are also home to hidden gems, such as hidden caves, natural springs, and ancient cart ruts etched into the limestone, offering glimpses into the island's prehistoric past.

The Maltese countryside beckons nature enthusiasts with its abundant flora and fauna. The island's rural areas are a sanctuary for migratory birds, such as kestrels and swallows, as well as indigenous species like the Maltese Wall Lizard. Exploring the countryside, one might encounter rabbits darting through fields or the occasional glimpse of a majestic falcon soaring overhead.

A stroll through the Maltese countryside is a sensory journey, where the beauty of nature intertwines with the essence of rural life. The songs of crickets, the fragrance of wild herbs, and the warm smiles of locals invite visitors to immerse themselves in the authenticity of Malta's heartland.

While the allure of Malta's historical sites and urban charm is undeniable, the countryside offers a different kind of enchantment - a tranquil retreat where time seems to stand still, and the connection with nature and tradition runs deep.

The Maltese countryside is a celebration of the island's soul, where the legacy of rural traditions and the splendor of nature harmoniously coexist. As visitors and locals alike traverse these bucolic landscapes, they become part of a timeless story, celebrating the beauty and richness of the Maltese countryside, a true haven of rural traditions and breathtaking landscapes.

Malta's Education System - Nurturing Knowledge and Talent

In the heart of the Mediterranean, Malta's commitment to education shines as a beacon of hope and progress for its people. The island's education system is a testament to its enduring dedication to nurturing knowledge and talent, empowering the young minds of Malta to shape a brighter future.

Education in Malta is compulsory for children between the ages of 5 and 16, ensuring that every child has access to the tools they need to unlock their full potential. The Ministry for Education and Employment oversees the nation's education policies and initiatives, aiming to provide a well-rounded and inclusive learning experience for all students.

Malta's education system is structured into three main stages: primary education, secondary education, and tertiary education. Primary education serves as the foundation, laying the groundwork for children's academic and personal development. Students typically attend primary school for six years, where they engage in a broad curriculum that includes language, mathematics, science, and social studies.

Upon completing primary education, students progress to secondary school, where they receive a more specialized education. Secondary education lasts for another six years, comprising two cycles: the Junior Cycle and the Senior Cycle. During the Junior Cycle, students continue their studies in core subjects while also exploring optional subjects that cater to their interests and talents.

At the end of the Junior Cycle, students sit for the Secondary Education Certificate (SEC) examinations, a crucial milestone that determines their progression to the Senior Cycle. The Senior Cycle offers students the option to pursue either academic or vocational pathways, catering to their diverse aspirations and career goals.

The General Certificate of Education Advanced Level (GCE A-Level) examinations mark the end of secondary education and pave the way for higher education opportunities. Students who excel in their A-Level exams may qualify for tertiary education institutions, both within Malta and internationally, where they can pursue specialized fields of study.

Malta takes pride in its network of state-funded and private schools, providing a high standard of education to its students. In recent years, the country has focused on modernizing its education infrastructure, investing in technology and resources to enhance the learning experience.

As Malta embraces the digital age, technology integration in classrooms has become a priority, equipping students with essential digital skills and preparing them for an increasingly interconnected world. The government's Digital Literacy Strategy emphasizes the use of technology to enrich teaching and learning, fostering a generation of digitally savvy individuals.

Language plays a significant role in Malta's education system. English and Maltese are both official languages, and instruction is delivered in both languages. English is taught as a subject from an early age, allowing students to develop fluency in this global language. Additionally, students study Maltese, preserving the island's cultural heritage and nurturing a sense of national identity.

Inclusivity and diversity are fundamental values in Malta's education system. Schools cater to students with special educational needs, providing tailored support and resources to ensure that every child receives an inclusive education. Efforts are also made to accommodate students from different cultural backgrounds, fostering a welcoming and nurturing learning environment.

Beyond academics, Malta's education system emphasizes the importance of extracurricular activities and the arts. Students are encouraged to explore their passions and talents in sports, music, drama, and various clubs and organizations. These activities not only enrich the learning experience but also foster a sense of camaraderie and personal growth.

The dedication and passion of Malta's educators play a pivotal role in shaping the success of its education system. Teachers are highly regarded in Maltese society, and their commitment to nurturing the next generation is celebrated by students, parents, and the community.

Malta's education system is a true celebration of knowledge, talent, and the pursuit of excellence. As the island invests in the education of its youth, it paves the way for a bright future, where innovation, creativity, and critical thinking thrive. From the classrooms to the corridors of academia, Malta's commitment to nurturing knowledge and talent is a testament to its enduring spirit of progress and its unwavering belief in the power of education to transform lives and shape a prosperous nation.

Traditional Maltese Crafts and Artisans - Keeping Heritage Alive

In the heart of the Mediterranean lies a treasure trove of cultural heritage, where traditional Maltese crafts and skilled artisans breathe life into age-old traditions. As the island of Malta embraces modernity, these artisans stand as custodians of the past, preserving and celebrating their craft with unwavering dedication, ensuring that the island's rich heritage remains vibrant and alive.

The art of lace-making, known as "bizzilla" in Maltese, is one of the most cherished traditional crafts on the island. Lace-making has been an integral part of Maltese culture since the 16th century, with intricate patterns and delicate designs passed down from generation to generation. Maltese lace is characterized by its fine threadwork and ornate motifs, with each piece reflecting the artisan's creativity and skill. Today, dedicated artisans continue to produce exquisite lace items, from tablecloths to clothing, perpetuating a craft that celebrates timeless elegance.

Pottery is another ancient craft that thrives in Malta. The island's rich clay deposits have provided artisans with the raw materials to create pottery for centuries. Traditional Maltese pottery is recognized for its earthy colors and rustic charm. Artisans mold clay into various shapes, including plates, vases, and decorative items, often embellishing them with hand-painted patterns inspired by the island's natural beauty. The craft of pottery not only serves as a testament to Malta's cultural heritage but also as a connection to the land from which the raw materials are sourced.

Woodcarving is a craft that showcases the talents of Maltese artisans who transform wood into intricately carved masterpieces. The craft of woodcarving holds a deep-rooted significance, with artisans often drawing inspiration from Malta's religious and historical symbolism. From beautifully carved wooden statues found in churches to ornate furniture gracing traditional Maltese homes, woodcarving remains a cherished art form that celebrates the island's identity.

Silver filigree, or "taraġ" in Maltese, is a captivating craft that exemplifies the meticulous artistry of Maltese artisans. Silver filigree is the delicate art of twisting and weaving thin silver wires into exquisite jewelry and decorative pieces. This intricate technique has been practiced in Malta for centuries, and artisans continue to create breathtaking filigree items, ranging from intricately designed earrings to ornate pendants. Each filigree piece is a testament to the artisan's dedication to preserving this ancient craft.

Maltese "qubbajt" or nougat is a sweet treat that has been enjoyed for generations. Made from honey, sugar, and almonds, this traditional confectionery is handcrafted by skilled artisans who follow time-honored recipes. Nougat-making has become a beloved tradition in Malta, especially during festive occasions such as Christmas and weddings, where this delectable treat is shared and celebrated with joy.

Basket weaving, known as "frgħana" in Maltese, is an age-old craft that showcases the island's resourcefulness and connection to nature. Artisans gather dried palm leaves, reeds, and other natural materials to create a variety of woven items, including baskets, bags, and decorative pieces. This sustainable craft not only pays homage to the island's rural traditions but also reflects the deep respect for nature and its resources.

The craft of "ganutell," delicate handmade flowers created from wire and beads, is an art form that has been cherished in Malta for centuries. Ganutell artisans meticulously craft these intricate flowers, which are often used to adorn bridal bouquets, religious statues, and traditional Maltese feasts. The art of ganutell exemplifies the patience and precision of Maltese artisans who continue to keep this delicate craft alive.

Malta's traditional crafts and the skilled artisans who practice them are a living testament to the island's cultural heritage. These crafts not only preserve the customs and traditions of the past but also serve as a source of pride for the Maltese people. As visitors and locals alike admire these handcrafted masterpieces, they become part of a timeless story that celebrates the ingenuity and creativity of the artisans who keep Malta's heritage alive.

Malta's Economy - From Agriculture to Financial Services

Nestled in the Mediterranean Sea, Malta's economy is a testament to the island's resilience, adaptability, and entrepreneurial spirit. Over the centuries, Malta's economic landscape has evolved, transforming from a primarily agrarian society to a diverse and thriving modern economy.

Historically, agriculture played a pivotal role in Malta's economy, with the cultivation of crops such as wheat, barley, and olives dating back to ancient times. The island's fertile soil and favorable climate supported agricultural practices that sustained the local population. However, as Malta underwent industrialization and urbanization in the 19th and 20th centuries, the agricultural sector gradually declined in importance.

Today, while agriculture remains a part of Malta's economy, it no longer holds the same prominence as it once did. Instead, Malta has diversified its economic activities, harnessing its strategic geographical location to become a hub for trade, services, and manufacturing.

The manufacturing sector in Malta has grown significantly, with industries such as pharmaceuticals, electronics, and precision engineering leading the way. Foreign direct investment has played a crucial role in boosting the manufacturing sector, attracting multinational companies to establish production facilities on the island.

Furthermore, Malta's strategic location has made it a vital player in international trade and logistics. The island's deep-water ports and well-connected airports facilitate the smooth movement of goods and services, enabling Malta to serve as a gateway between Europe, Africa, and the Middle East.

In recent decades, Malta has emerged as a prominent player in the financial services sector. The country's proactive approach to financial regulation and attractive tax incentives have drawn international companies to set up offices on the island. Malta's financial services industry encompasses banking, insurance, asset management, and fintech, contributing significantly to the country's GDP.

Tourism is another cornerstone of Malta's economy, drawing millions of visitors each year to experience the island's rich history, stunning landscapes, and vibrant culture. The tourism industry has expanded to cater to diverse travelers, offering a wide range of accommodations, dining experiences, and leisure activities.

As a member of the European Union (EU), Malta benefits from access to the EU's single market, providing opportunities for trade and investment across the region. The country's adoption of the Euro as its currency has further strengthened its economic ties with Europe.

Malta's small and open economy is characterized by its resilience and adaptability. Despite facing challenges, such as its limited natural resources and vulnerability to global economic fluctuations, the country has shown remarkable tenacity in navigating economic waters.

The government of Malta has played a proactive role in promoting economic growth and development. Initiatives to support entrepreneurship, innovation, and research and development have fostered a dynamic business environment, encouraging startups and established businesses alike to flourish.

In recent years, the digital economy has gained momentum in Malta, with the government actively promoting the growth of the ICT (Information and Communication Technology) sector. The establishment of technology parks and the provision of incentives for tech companies have attracted investments and talent in the digital domain.

Additionally, Malta has placed a strong emphasis on education and skills development to nurture a workforce equipped for the demands of a modern economy. The country's educational institutions collaborate closely with the private sector to ensure that graduates possess the skills needed to contribute to various industries.

Malta's economic journey is a tale of transformation and progress. From its agrarian roots to its current status as a dynamic player in the global economy, the island's spirit of innovation and determination has paved the way for its economic success. As Malta continues to embrace new opportunities and navigate challenges, it remains a beacon of economic resilience and celebrates the diverse tapestry of industries that contribute to its thriving economy.

The Maltese Flag and National Symbols - Significance and Evolution

In the heart of the Mediterranean Sea, the Maltese flag proudly unfurls, representing the island's rich history, culture, and identity. As a nation with a storied past and a vibrant present, Malta's national symbols hold deep significance, serving as a powerful reflection of its people's unity and resilience.

The Maltese flag features a striking design, with two vertical bands of white and red, and a representation of the George Cross in the upper hoist corner. The George Cross, a silver cross, is a prestigious award bestowed upon Malta by King George VI of the United Kingdom in recognition of the island's extraordinary bravery and fortitude during World War II. This honor, given on April 15, 1942, marked the first time an entire nation was recognized for its collective gallantry. The white color on the flag symbolizes peace and purity, embodying the hope for a harmonious and tranquil society. The red color, on the other hand, signifies bravery and sacrifice, a tribute to the valor and determination of the Maltese people throughout their history. The juxtaposition of these colors creates a visually striking flag, evoking a sense of national pride and unity. Beyond the flag, Malta boasts several other national symbols that carry significant cultural and historical meanings. The national emblem, known as the "Coat of Arms of Malta," is an intricate design that features a heraldic shield flanked by two dolphins. The shield portrays a golden mural crown on a blue background, representing Malta's fortress-like status and its connection to the sea. The national motto "Repubblika ta' Malta" (Republic of Malta) is inscribed below the shield, reaffirming the country's sovereign status. The Maltese national animal, the Pharaoh Hound, is a beloved and ancient breed known for its agility, grace, and loyalty. Recognizable by its sleek, tan coat and unique "blushing" trait (where its nose and ears turn pink when excited), the Pharaoh Hound has been associated with Malta for centuries. It is often considered a symbol of the island's heritage and has been celebrated in various forms of art and literature.

The Maltese national flower is the Maltese Centaury (Cheirolophus crassifolius), a vibrant and rare purple flower that thrives in the island's rocky landscapes. This resilient flower has come to represent Malta's tenacity and ability to bloom even in the harshest conditions. The Maltese Cross is another emblem deeply ingrained in the nation's identity. Originating from the Knights Hospitaller, a religious military order that played a significant role in Malta's history, the eight-pointed cross symbolizes the values of charity, loyalty, and courage. Today, the Maltese Cross is used in various contexts, from military insignia to civil service emblems, and continues to evoke a sense of honor and duty.

Throughout history, Malta's national symbols have evolved, reflecting the island's journey through various eras and influences. From the ancient civilizations that once graced its shores to the Knights of St. John and beyond, each chapter of Malta's history has left its mark on its national symbols. The enduring significance of these symbols is evident in their frequent use in everyday life. From official government documents to street signs and postage stamps, Malta's national symbols are proudly displayed, instilling a sense of identity and unity among its people.

Malta's Ancient Cart Ruts - A Mystery in Stone

Nestled on the sun-kissed island of Malta lie enigmatic and ancient cart ruts, a fascinating archaeological wonder that has puzzled researchers and captivated the imagination of locals and visitors alike. These enigmatic tracks etched into the island's limestone terrain are a testament to a mysterious past, shrouded in the mists of time, and continue to evoke wonder and curiosity.

The cart ruts, known as "karren" in Maltese, form an intricate network of parallel tracks, measuring around 60 centimeters wide, carved into the rock surface. They meander across the Maltese landscape, stretching across hills, valleys, and even cliffsides, spanning vast distances. The remarkable precision and straightness of the ruts, despite the rugged terrain, have led some to speculate that they were the product of advanced engineering techniques.

Scholars and archaeologists have debated the origins and purpose of the cart ruts for decades, but no definitive explanation has been reached. Numerous theories abound, each offering intriguing possibilities. One prevailing hypothesis suggests that the ruts were created during the Bronze Age, around 2000 to 2500 BCE, as pathways for transporting heavy stone blocks to construct megalithic temples.

Malta's megalithic temples, such as the UNESCO-listed Ħaġar Qim and Mnajdra temples, are some of the world's oldest freestanding structures. The cart ruts, found in proximity to these temples, have led researchers to believe that they may have served as tracks for transporting the massive stones used in temple construction. The precision of the ruts is particularly striking, hinting at a sophisticated system of transportation used by the ancient inhabitants of Malta.

Another theory posits that the cart ruts were formed by large sledges or carts used for agricultural purposes, such as transporting crops or livestock across the island. This theory gains support from the presence of the cart ruts in agricultural areas, where the parallel tracks would have facilitated efficient transportation and reduced soil erosion.

Despite the lack of definitive answers, the cart ruts have become an integral part of Malta's cultural heritage and have captured the imagination of artists, writers, and storytellers. Some local legends associate the cart ruts with supernatural beings or divine intervention, infusing these ancient tracks with a sense of mystique and wonder.

In 1986, an archaeological study led by David H. Trump suggested that the cart ruts might have been channels used for directing water from springs to agricultural fields, serving a vital role in sustaining the island's agriculture during ancient times. This irrigation theory adds another layer of complexity to the mystery, as it hints at the multi-functional nature of the cart ruts and their crucial role in the island's survival.

To this day, the cart ruts of Malta continue to intrigue experts and enthusiasts, prompting ongoing research and investigations into their origins and purpose. Their presence enriches Malta's cultural landscape, underscoring the island's deep-rooted history and its connection to its prehistoric past.

The Maltese people take pride in these ancient cart ruts, celebrating their enigmatic beauty and embracing their role as custodians of a captivating historical legacy. As the cart ruts stand as silent witnesses to an ancient era, they beckon visitors to ponder the mysteries of the past, inviting them on a journey of exploration and discovery.

While the precise origins of the cart ruts may remain shrouded in mystery, their enduring presence on the island of Malta is a testament to the lasting impact of its ancient inhabitants. These intricate stone tracks not only connect the present to the past but also spark the imagination and curiosity of all who encounter them, weaving a timeless narrative that celebrates the enigma and allure of Malta's ancient cart ruts, a captivating mystery etched in stone.

The Maltese Falcon - A Literary Icon and Its Connections

In the realm of literature, there exists an enduring and enigmatic figure that has captivated readers for generations—the Maltese Falcon. This iconic masterpiece, penned by American author Dashiell Hammett, has left an indelible mark on the literary landscape and is deeply intertwined with the history and cultural fabric of Malta.

Published in 1930, "The Maltese Falcon" is a classic detective novel that introduced readers to the enigmatic and sharp-witted private investigator, Sam Spade. Set against the backdrop of 1920s San Francisco, the novel weaves a tale of intrigue, betrayal, and relentless pursuit, revolving around the search for a priceless statuette—the titular Maltese Falcon.

While the majority of the novel unfolds in the bustling streets of San Francisco, it is the mysterious and fabled Maltese Falcon that serves as the focal point of the narrative, drawing characters into its orbit like moths to a flame. The falcon itself, a statuette of a bird encrusted with precious jewels, symbolizes greed, deception, and the allure of the unknown.

But what connects this celebrated novel to the island of Malta, thousands of miles away in the Mediterranean Sea? The answer lies in the rich history and allure of the real-world Maltese Falcon, a connection that intertwines fact and fiction in a mesmerizing dance.

In reality, the Maltese Falcon is a historical artifact of great significance. The original statuette, however, is not a priceless jewel-encrusted falcon but a more humble and yet equally captivating gilded wooden carving. This intricate wooden falcon, believed to have been crafted in the 16th century, is a symbol of Malta's historical ties to the Order of the Knights Hospitaller, also known as the Knights of St. John.

The Knights Hospitaller, an ancient military order, played a pivotal role in Malta's history, and their legacy is deeply ingrained in the island's cultural heritage. It was during their rule in the 16th century that the Maltese Falcon became a cherished emblem of the island, representing the valor, chivalry, and unwavering faith of the knights.

The real-world Maltese Falcon is housed in the National Museum of Archaeology in Valletta, Malta's capital city. This captivating artifact serves as a tangible link between the literary world of Dashiell Hammett's novel and the historical tapestry of Malta.

The power of literature lies in its ability to transcend time and space, forging connections between seemingly disparate worlds. "The Maltese Falcon" does just that, weaving a literary tapestry that reaches across continents to embrace the island of Malta, its heritage, and its cherished historical artifacts.

In Malta, the legacy of "The Maltese Falcon" lives on, celebrated not only in the museum but also in the hearts and minds of the Maltese people. The novel's impact on popular culture endures, with film adaptations and references in various works paying homage to its enduring allure.

As readers continue to delve into the pages of "The Maltese Falcon," they embark on a journey that transcends time, culture, and geography. The novel's exploration of human nature, morality, and the allure of the unknown resonates with readers across generations, mirroring the timeless appeal of the real-world Maltese Falcon.

In this celebration of Malta, we recognize the island's capacity to inspire and be inspired, to forge connections between fiction and reality, and to hold a mirror to the complexities of the human spirit. "The Maltese Falcon" and its enigmatic connection to Malta stand as a testament to the power of literature to transcend borders and bridge the gaps between worlds, enriching our understanding of both fact and fiction, and inviting us to explore the mysteries that lie within the pages of a treasured literary icon.

The Megalithic Temples of Malta - UNESCO World Heritage Sites

On the idyllic island of Malta, amid the sun-kissed landscapes and azure waters of the Mediterranean Sea, stand the awe-inspiring Megalithic Temples. These remarkable architectural marvels, dating back to prehistoric times, hold the key to a fascinating and mysterious chapter in Malta's history, earning them the prestigious title of UNESCO World Heritage Sites.

The Megalithic Temples of Malta are a collection of ancient stone structures, unparalleled in their sophistication and grandeur. Constructed between 3600 and 2500 BCE, these temples predate both the Egyptian pyramids and England's Stonehenge, making them some of the world's oldest freestanding structures. Their sheer age and the precision of their construction have baffled archaeologists and scholars, sparking countless theories about the island's early inhabitants and their remarkable achievements.

The Megalithic Temples are scattered across the islands of Malta and Gozo, each site offering a glimpse into the ancient beliefs and rituals of the people who once called these lands home. The temples are characterized by massive stone blocks, meticulously carved and arranged to create intricate architectural wonders that continue to defy the test of time.

Among the most renowned Megalithic Temples in Malta is the Ġgantija complex on the island of Gozo. Dating back over 5,500 years, Ġgantija is one of the earliest and best-preserved temples, with its colossal stone walls rising majestically into the sky. The temple's name, meaning "giantess" in Maltese, alludes to the legendary belief that the temples were built by giants due to the monumental scale of their construction.

On the main island of Malta, the Ħaġar Qim and Mnajdra temples are two exceptional examples of the island's ancient architectural prowess. Perched on a rugged cliffside, these temples command breathtaking views of the Mediterranean Sea, further emphasizing the connection between the ancient builders and the natural world.

The Tarxien Temples, situated in the southeastern region of Malta, form yet another testament to the island's prehistoric past. The intricate carvings and symbolic patterns adorning the temple walls offer tantalizing clues about the spiritual beliefs and practices of the people who congregated within their sacred confines.

These temples, shrouded in the mists of antiquity, were not only places of worship but also central hubs for community gatherings and ceremonies. The vast and laborious efforts invested in their construction speak to the importance of religious and communal life during this era, as well as the impressive engineering knowledge possessed by their creators.

The Megalithic Temples of Malta have garnered global recognition for their historical and cultural significance. In 1980, UNESCO designated these temples as World Heritage Sites, acknowledging their universal value and the need to protect and preserve them for future generations.

Over the years, extensive conservation efforts have been undertaken to safeguard these ancient treasures. Modern technology and archaeological expertise have been harnessed to ensure that the temples remain intact, allowing visitors to experience the awe-inspiring wonder of stepping back in time to an era long past.

As a testament to Malta's rich cultural heritage, the Megalithic Temples continue to draw visitors from all corners of the globe. They stand not only as a source of national pride for the Maltese people but also as a bridge to understanding the enigmatic past of humanity as a whole.

The Megalithic Temples of Malta, with their enigmatic allure and timeless beauty, are a celebration of the island's ancient past and a testament to the ingenuity and spirituality of its early inhabitants. In their weathered stone walls, we glimpse the profound and enduring connection between humanity and the landscapes we inhabit, reminding us of the unbroken thread of history that weaves through the tapestry of Malta's story.

The Maltese Language - A Living Linguistic Treasure

Nestled in the heart of the Mediterranean Sea, Malta is a land of captivating beauty and rich cultural heritage. Among its many treasures lies a unique gem, the Maltese language, a linguistic marvel that stands as a living testament to the island's rich history and vibrant identity.

The Maltese language is the only Semitic language written in the Latin script, making it an extraordinary fusion of diverse linguistic influences. Its origins can be traced back to the arrival of the Phoenicians in Malta around 750 BCE, who left an indelible mark on the island's linguistic landscape. Over the centuries, waves of conquerors, traders, and settlers contributed to the linguistic tapestry, resulting in the dynamic and diverse language we know today.

At its core, the Maltese language is descended from a dialect of Arabic, infused with words from Italian, Sicilian, English, French, and Spanish, among others. This unique blend of influences has given rise to a rich vocabulary and a diverse array of expressions, reflecting the island's multicultural history and its interactions with various civilizations.

Despite its diverse linguistic heritage, Maltese remains firmly rooted in its Semitic origins. The grammar, syntax, and structure of the language are heavily influenced by Arabic, distinguishing it from other Romance languages spoken in neighboring countries.

One of the most fascinating aspects of the Maltese language is its resilience and evolution over time. Despite centuries of foreign domination and influence, the Maltese people have tenaciously preserved their native tongue, a testament to their deep sense of cultural identity and pride. Today, Maltese is recognized as an official language of Malta, alongside English.

The preservation and promotion of the Maltese language are supported by the Maltese government, which recognizes its importance as a symbol of national identity and cultural heritage. Schools across the island teach in both Maltese and English, ensuring that future generations continue to embrace and appreciate their linguistic legacy.

The Maltese language not only unites the people of Malta but also serves as a bridge to the past, connecting modern-day Malta with its ancient roots. The influence of Arabic, in particular, is evident in everyday phrases, expressions, and proverbs, providing a glimpse into the island's historical interactions with Arab traders and settlers.

Beyond the spoken word, Maltese literature plays a vital role in preserving and celebrating the language. Renowned Maltese authors and poets have contributed to a rich literary tradition, producing works that reflect the unique nuances and expressive power of the language.

In recent years, efforts have been made to promote the Maltese language on a global stage. Online resources, language courses, and cultural exchange programs have enabled non-Maltese speakers to delve into the beauty and intricacies of this unique linguistic treasure.

The Maltese language is more than just a means of communication; it is a source of pride, unity, and cultural heritage for the Maltese people. It reflects their resilience, adaptability, and openness to the world, qualities that have shaped the island's history and continue to define its future.

World War II and Malta's Heroic Resistance

In the annals of history, few episodes shine as brightly as Malta's heroic resistance during World War II. As the Mediterranean island found itself at the crossroads of conflict, its people displayed unwavering courage, resilience, and determination in the face of relentless adversity. During the dark days of the war, Malta emerged as a beacon of hope and an indomitable fortress, earning the admiration and respect of allies and adversaries alike.

At the outbreak of World War II in 1939, Malta was a British colony strategically positioned between Europe and North Africa. Its location made it a coveted prize for Axis powers seeking to control the Mediterranean Sea. Recognizing the island's significance, Adolf Hitler and Benito Mussolini set their sights on Malta, intent on breaking the British stronghold and gaining a vital foothold in the Mediterranean.

The heroic resistance of Malta began in earnest in 1940 when Italy, under Mussolini's command, launched an intensive aerial campaign aimed at crippling the island's defenses. The Italian Air Force, or Regia Aeronautica, bombarded Malta with unrelenting ferocity, targeting both military installations and civilian areas. The people of Malta, however, stood resolute in the face of the relentless barrage, displaying a remarkable spirit of defiance that would come to define their wartime legacy.

As the Italian assault intensified, the plight of Malta drew international attention. Winston Churchill, the British Prime Minister, recognized the strategic significance of the island and declared, "Malta is the key to the war." The valiant resistance of the Maltese people and the British garrison stationed on the island earned Malta the George Cross, a prestigious award for civilian gallantry, making it the only entire country to receive such an honor.

In April 1941, as the Axis powers increased their onslaught, Hitler ordered the Luftwaffe, the German Air Force, to join the attack on Malta. What followed was a harrowing period known as the "Siege of Malta." The island endured incessant bombing raids that targeted crucial ports, airfields, and supply routes. Food and medical supplies became scarce, and the island's population faced dire conditions.

Yet, despite the tremendous hardships, Malta's resolve never wavered. The Maltese people, along with British servicemen and women, endured the relentless bombardment with unwavering courage. They sought refuge in underground shelters, known as "the Malta rock caves," and faced danger and deprivation with a sense of unity that transcended all divides.

Throughout the Siege of Malta, a steady stream of supplies, including crucial fuel and ammunition, were ferried to the island by British convoys, braving the perilous Mediterranean Sea under constant threat from enemy aircraft and U-boats. These daring and often treacherous resupply missions, codenamed "Operation Pedestal," played a pivotal role in sustaining Malta's resistance and securing its survival.

The turning point for Malta came in 1942, when the tide of the war began to shift in favor of the Allies. The crucial victory in the Battle of El Alamein, led by General Bernard

Montgomery in North Africa, weakened the Axis hold on the region and provided vital breathing space for the beleaguered island.

As the Allies gained the upper hand, the intensity of the Axis bombardment gradually subsided. In November 1942, King George VI of Britain visited Malta to honor the island's extraordinary bravery and present the George Cross. The visit bolstered the morale of the Maltese people, reaffirming their crucial role in the broader struggle for freedom.

The Siege of Malta officially ended on November 20, 1942, marking a decisive triumph of resilience and determination over overwhelming odds. The heroic resistance of Malta had foiled the Axis plans to capture the island and secure control of the Mediterranean, dealing a significant blow to the enemy's war efforts.

Malta emerged from World War II scarred but triumphant, a living testament to the unyielding human spirit and the power of collective courage. Its heroic resistance earned the island a place in history as a symbol of hope, tenacity, and unwavering commitment to liberty.

Today, the legacy of Malta's heroic resistance lives on in the hearts of the Maltese people and resonates across the globe. Visitors to the island can explore the remnants of its wartime past, including the vast network of underground shelters and the historic sites that bear witness to the island's indomitable spirit.

Exploring Malta's Caves and Grottoes - Nature's Hidden Gems

Beneath the sun-drenched landscapes and ancient temples of Malta lie a mesmerizing network of caves and grottoes, a hidden world of natural wonders waiting to be explored. These underground marvels have been shaped over millennia by the forces of nature, and they hold within them a treasure trove of geological and historical secrets.

The Maltese islands, with their limestone geology, boast a wealth of caves and grottoes that have been formed through the intricate interplay of rainwater and the island's porous rock. Over time, these geological processes have carved out majestic chambers, intricate passageways, and breathtaking stalactite formations, creating an underground realm of unparalleled beauty.

One of Malta's most renowned caves is the Għar Dalam, located in the southeastern part of the main island. Its name translates to "Cave of Darkness," and within its depths lies a rich fossil record that spans thousands of years. The cave's sediment layers have preserved the remains of prehistoric animals, including pygmy elephants, hippopotami, and deer, providing invaluable insights into Malta's ancient ecological history.

Another fascinating cave complex is the Għar Ħasan, found on the outskirts of the village of Birżebbuġa. This labyrinthine system of caves captivates visitors with its striking stalactite formations and captivating rock formations that resemble cascading waterfalls frozen in time. The ethereal ambiance within Għar Ħasan conjures a sense of wonder and mystery, inviting visitors to contemplate the eons of natural processes that have shaped its unique landscape.

In the northwestern part of the main island, the Blue Grotto is a natural wonder that dazzles with its iridescent blue waters and sheer limestone cliffs. Boat tours allow visitors to sail through the grotto's sea caverns, where sunlight refracts through the water, creating an otherworldly azure glow. The Blue Grotto is a testament to the awe-inspiring beauty that lies beneath Malta's azure waves.

A visit to the underground realm of the Ġgantija Temples in Gozo unveils the wonders of the Xagħra Stone Circle, an impressive ancient rock formation believed to have been used by the temple builders for ritualistic purposes. The site's mystique and enigmatic aura hint at its possible role in the island's prehistoric spiritual practices.

The mystical allure of Malta's caves and grottoes extends beyond their geological beauty; many of these subterranean sanctuaries have historical and cultural significance as well. Over the centuries, these hidden chambers have served as shelters, hiding places, and even places of worship during times of conflict and adversity.

Throughout Malta's long history, these caves and grottoes have played a role in local folklore and legends, woven into tales of fantastical creatures and mythical beings that have captured the imagination of generations. The island's rich tapestry of legends includes stories of giants, goblins, and supernatural beings who are said to have inhabited these mystical underground realms.

Today, the exploration of Malta's caves and grottoes has become an integral part of the island's eco-tourism and adventure activities. Local tour operators offer guided excursions, allowing visitors to venture deep into the heart of these geological wonders, revealing the hidden beauty of Malta's subterranean world.

Exploring Malta's caves and grottoes is not only an opportunity to witness the wonders of nature but also a chance to connect with the island's ancient past. These subterranean sanctuaries remind us of the intricate interplay between humans and the natural world throughout history, as well as the enduring power of nature's creative forces.

The Maltese Fishing Tradition - Sustaining a Way of Life

As the Mediterranean sun casts its warm embrace upon the shores of Malta, the island's timeless fishing tradition comes to life. For centuries, fishing has been an integral part of Maltese culture, shaping the way of life for coastal communities and connecting them intimately with the bountiful sea that surrounds them. This chapter celebrates the enduring legacy of the Maltese fishing tradition, a cherished heritage that sustains both livelihoods and a deep-rooted cultural identity.

The history of fishing in Malta stretches back to ancient times, with evidence of fishing practices dating as far back as the Phoenician and Roman eras. These early seafarers recognized the abundant marine resources of the Mediterranean and harnessed them as a vital source of sustenance. The fishing tradition passed down through generations, becoming an intrinsic part of the island's fabric and heritage.

Traditional Maltese fishing techniques have been honed over centuries of experience, reflecting a deep understanding of the sea and its seasonal rhythms. The iconic Maltese fishing boats, known as "luzzus," are instantly recognizable with their vibrant colors, intricately painted eyes, and sturdy design. These sturdy vessels are crafted by skilled boat builders using techniques handed down through generations, ensuring that each luzzu is a work of art as well as a functional tool for the trade.

Fishing in Malta is a family affair, with knowledge and skills passed down from fathers to sons, and mothers to daughters. This intergenerational transmission of expertise ensures the continuity of the fishing tradition and the preservation of time-honored techniques. As the sun rises over the horizon, the Maltese fishermen set sail, guided by their intimate knowledge of the sea and its currents.

The bounty of the Mediterranean provides a diverse array of fish and seafood, and the Maltese fishing tradition celebrates sustainability and responsible harvesting. Practices such as the use of traditional fishing nets, line fishing, and handline techniques demonstrate the respect for the delicate marine ecosystem and the need to preserve it for future generations.

Fishermen in Malta exhibit a profound connection to their craft, often spending long hours at sea, braving unpredictable weather and rough seas. Their commitment and dedication reflect the deeply ingrained appreciation for the ocean and the life it sustains. The catch is often brought ashore to bustling fish markets, where the freshest seafood is proudly displayed, offering a glimpse into the rich marine bounty of the Mediterranean.

Beyond its economic significance, the Maltese fishing tradition holds cultural and social importance. Fishermen are revered members of their communities, celebrated for their bravery, hard work, and the vital role they play in providing nourishment for the island. Fishermen's feasts, or "festi tal-pizzi," are vibrant celebrations that honor the patron saint of fishermen, St. Peter, with joyous processions, traditional music, and delectable seafood feasts.

In recent years, the challenges of modernization and changing fishing practices have impacted the traditional fishing community in Malta. However, efforts have been made to preserve and promote the ancient fishing traditions, recognizing their value not only in terms of sustenance but also as an integral part of the island's cultural heritage.

Today, the Maltese fishing tradition thrives as a symbol of resilience, cultural identity, and sustainable practices. The fishermen of Malta carry on the legacy of their forefathers, exemplifying the deep-rooted connection between the island's people and the sea that has sustained them for millennia.

Astronomy in Malta - Ancient Observatories and Contemporary Endeavors

Nestled in the heart of the Mediterranean, Malta has long been a land of celestial fascination, where the skies have beckoned humanity to explore the mysteries of the cosmos. From ancient times to the present day, the island has embraced the wonders of astronomy, nurturing a profound connection between its people and the celestial realms above. This chapter celebrates the rich tapestry of astronomy in Malta, encompassing the legacy of ancient observatories and the vibrant contemporary endeavors that continue to kindle a passion for the stars.

As far back as 4,000 years ago, the ancient inhabitants of Malta gazed upon the heavens with awe and wonder. The prehistoric temples of Ġgantija and Mnajdra on the island of Gozo, and Ħaġar Qim and Mnajdra on the main island, are architectural marvels meticulously aligned with the solstices and equinoxes. These remarkable megalithic structures served not only as places of worship but also as celestial observatories, allowing the ancient Maltese to chart the movements of the sun, stars, and planets with astonishing precision.

The Neolithic cart ruts found across the Maltese landscape have also sparked astronomical interest. Some researchers propose that these enigmatic tracks, carved into the rock, may have served as ancient astronomical markers, further illuminating the island's early fascination with the celestial realm.

Fast forward to the medieval era, and Malta's connection with astronomy continued to flourish. The Knights of St. John, who made the island their home during the Middle Ages, were known for their scholarly pursuits, including the study of astronomy. The Grand Master's Palace in Valletta, which now houses the Office of the President of Malta, was once a hub of astronomical observation and learning.

In the 17th century, Maltese astronomer Giovanni Antonio Cassarotti made significant contributions to the field. He was a member of the prestigious Accademia dei Lincei in Rome, founded by Federico Cesi and Galileo Galilei, and his research on comets and celestial phenomena earned him recognition among the leading astronomers of his time.

Fast forward again to modern times, and astronomy in Malta has entered a new and exciting era. The island boasts a strong community of astronomers, amateur stargazers, and science enthusiasts who regularly gather to marvel at the night skies. Events such as "Astronomy on the Move" and "Starry Nights Malta" engage the public and ignite a sense of wonder about the cosmos.

Malta's clear skies and low light pollution make it an ideal location for stargazing and celestial observation. The Maltese countryside, with its serene landscapes, offers the perfect backdrop for contemplating the vastness of the universe. This allure has even attracted international organizations and researchers seeking dark sky locations for their astronomical pursuits.

In recent years, Malta's efforts in promoting astronomy and space science have grown. The Malta Council for Science and Technology (MCST) has been instrumental in fostering collaborations with international space agencies and research institutions, opening doors to cutting-edge astronomical research and educational initiatives.

In recognition of its commitment to exploring the cosmos, Malta has become an associate member of the European Southern Observatory (ESO). This partnership offers Maltese astronomers and researchers access to world-class telescopes and observational facilities, further advancing the island's contribution to the field of astronomy.

The allure of astronomy in Malta extends beyond its borders. The island's potential as a hub for space and astronomical tourism has garnered attention from the international space community. As interest in space travel and celestial exploration grows, Malta stands poised to play an active role in these extraordinary endeavors.

Malta's Unique Transportation - From Traditional "Dghajsa" to Modern Ferries

Amidst the picturesque Mediterranean backdrop, Malta's transportation system weaves a fascinating tale of innovation, tradition, and adaptability. The island's unique blend of ancient and modern modes of transport reflects its dynamic history and cosmopolitan spirit. From the traditional "dghajsa" boats gliding gracefully across the Grand Harbour to the state-of-the-art ferries connecting the islands, this chapter celebrates the diversity and charm of Malta's transportation heritage.

One of the most iconic and cherished symbols of Maltese transportation is the "dghajsa," a traditional wooden boat with a distinctive pointed bow and elegant lines. Historically, these watercraft were essential for fishing and transporting goods around the islands. Today, "dghajsa" rides offer a leisurely and scenic way to traverse Malta's harbors, with skilled boatmen known as "tal-lettax" guiding visitors through the azure waters of the Grand Harbour.

The "dghajsa" tradition dates back to the time of the Knights of St. John, who recognized the practicality and versatility of these boats for maritime activities. These small vessels allowed the Knights to move efficiently through the narrow and crowded waterways of the harbors.

While the "dghajsa" serves as a charming reminder of Malta's maritime past, the island's modern transportation infrastructure has evolved to meet the demands of contemporary life. Malta's public bus service, operated by the Transport Malta agency, is an extensive network that connects the various regions of the main island, Gozo, and Comino. The bright yellow buses are a familiar sight on the roads, offering an affordable and convenient mode of travel for locals and visitors alike.

Complementing the bus service, the introduction of the Malta Public Transport mobile app has made navigating the island's bus routes even more accessible. Travelers can now plan their journeys, track bus arrivals in real-time, and access essential information with just a few taps on their smartphones.

Beyond land transport, Malta's maritime connections are equally vital to its transportation network. The Malta-Gozo ferry service, operated by Gozo Channel Company, links the main island to Gozo, making the enchanting sister island easily accessible for tourists and residents. The ferry journey offers breathtaking views of Malta's coastline and the imposing Citadella, perched atop the hills of Victoria, Gozo's capital.

For visitors who wish to explore the islands from a different perspective, a network of modern and efficient water taxis is available. These water taxis connect various points around Malta, including popular destinations such as Valletta, Sliema, and St. Julian's. The water taxi service offers not only convenience but also a delightful way to experience the beauty of Malta's coastline.

Additionally, Malta's harbor area offers opportunities for harbor cruises and boat tours, enabling tourists to explore the islands' scenic beauty from a different vantage point. These excursions showcase the stunning architecture of Valletta, the majestic Three Cities, and the remarkable natural beauty of the Blue Grotto.

In recent years, Malta has embraced sustainable transportation initiatives as part of its commitment to environmental responsibility. The introduction of electric scooters and bicycles for rent in urban areas has provided eco-friendly alternatives for short-distance travel, reducing carbon emissions and easing traffic congestion.

As the island continues to grow and evolve, Malta's transportation system adapts and innovates, seamlessly blending tradition with progress. The coexistence of the traditional "dghajsa" and the modern ferries, buses, and water taxis symbolizes the island's ability to preserve its cultural heritage while embracing the benefits of technological advancements.

Malta's Future - Preserving the Past, Embracing the Future

As the sun sets over the enchanting Maltese archipelago, a sense of hope and determination lingers in the air—a spirit that has defined the Maltese people throughout their storied history. Looking ahead to Malta's future, there is an unwavering commitment to preserving the island's rich past while embracing the boundless opportunities that lie on the horizon. This chapter celebrates Malta's future, where the threads of heritage and progress are intricately woven together, creating a tapestry of promise and possibility.

One of the cornerstones of Malta's future lies in its commitment to preserving its treasured past. The UNESCO World Heritage Sites scattered across the islands, from the ancient megalithic temples to the stunning architecture of Valletta, stand as testaments to Malta's enduring cultural heritage. These sites not only serve as points of pride for the Maltese people but also draw visitors from around the world, contributing to the island's vibrant tourism industry.

Malta's commitment to safeguarding its heritage is evident through ongoing restoration and conservation efforts. Renowned historical landmarks, such as St. John's Co-Cathedral and the Ħal Saflieni Hypogeum, undergo meticulous restoration, ensuring that future generations can continue to marvel at their beauty and significance.

Education plays a pivotal role in shaping Malta's future, with a focus on nurturing knowledge and talent. The island boasts a robust education system, providing a solid foundation for students to explore their passions and talents. Institutions such as the University of Malta offer a wide range of academic disciplines and research opportunities, attracting international students and fostering collaboration with global academic networks.

In the realm of science and technology, Malta is making strides to become a hub of innovation and research. Initiatives by the Malta Council for Science and Technology (MCST) and collaborations with international organizations propel the island forward in areas such as space exploration, renewable energy, and artificial intelligence.

Sustainability is a driving force in Malta's future aspirations. The island is acutely aware of its environmental responsibilities and is actively adopting greener practices. Initiatives to reduce plastic waste, promote renewable energy, and preserve the delicate marine ecosystem are key components of Malta's sustainable development strategy.

As a small island nation, Malta understands the significance of international cooperation and global partnerships. The island is an active member of the European Union and the United Nations, contributing to international dialogues and advocating for global issues such as climate change and sustainable development.

Malta's future is intrinsically linked to its strategic geographical location. The island's role as a bridge between Europe, Africa, and the Middle East positions it as a significant player in international trade, tourism, and diplomacy.

The tourism industry, a pillar of Malta's economy, continues to thrive with an emphasis on providing authentic and immersive experiences. As the world looks to travel responsibly and sustainably, Malta's diverse attractions, rich cultural heritage, and picturesque landscapes position it as a coveted destination.

In a world increasingly interconnected by technology, Malta's future embraces digital innovation. The island is harnessing the power of the digital age to enhance services, improve infrastructure, and foster e-governance, ensuring that Malta remains at the forefront of the digital revolution.

Malta's future celebrates the spirit of entrepreneurship and economic diversification. The island nurtures a thriving startup ecosystem, attracting innovators and investors seeking new opportunities in emerging industries.

Above all, the Maltese people are the driving force behind the island's promising future. Their resilience, creativity, and passion for their homeland ensure that Malta will continue to flourish and evolve in the years to come.

In celebrating Malta's future, we celebrate the enduring spirit of a nation that cherishes its past while forging a path towards a brighter and more sustainable tomorrow. As the sun rises on the horizon, illuminating the Maltese landscape, it symbolizes the dawn of a new era—a future that preserves the essence of Malta's heritage while embracing the limitless possibilities that await.

Epilogue

As we conclude our journey through the enchanting tales of Malta, a sense of wonder and admiration lingers in our hearts. The island's rich history, vibrant culture, and breathtaking landscapes have left an indelible mark on our souls. Malta's enduring allure as a destination that celebrates its past while embracing the future beckons us to return time and time again.

Throughout our exploration of Malta, we have encountered a land steeped in ancient mysteries and storied legends. From the megalithic temples that stand as silent witnesses to prehistoric civilizations, to the medieval legacy of the Knights of St. John, every step reveals a tapestry of human endeavor and ingenuity.

The Maltese people, with their warm hospitality and vibrant spirit, have welcomed us into their world with open arms. Their traditions, customs, and festivals have given us a glimpse into their cultural identity, forging a connection that transcends geographical boundaries.

Malta's architectural marvels, from the Baroque masterpieces of Valletta to the time-worn walls of Mdina, have provided a window into the island's illustrious past. The grand capital city, Valletta, with its imposing fortifications and majestic Grand Harbour, stands as a testament to Malta's resilience and fortitude throughout centuries of challenges.

The Maltese countryside, with its rural traditions and breathtaking landscapes, has shown us the harmony between nature and humanity. As we explored the hidden gems of caves and grottoes, we marveled at the beauty that lies beneath the surface, mirroring the captivating stories that lie within the hearts of the Maltese people.

Amidst the serenity of the Mediterranean Sea, we embarked on journeys aboard traditional "dghajsa" boats, tracing the footsteps of ancient mariners and embracing the legacy of maritime heritage. And as we sailed on modern ferries, we admired how Malta's future is anchored in preserving its treasured past while charting new horizons.

Malta's cuisine, a gastronomic adventure of flavors, tantalized our taste buds with its fusion of Mediterranean influences. From the humble delights of pastizzi to the delectable seafood dishes, every meal was a celebration of the island's culinary diversity.

The Maltese language, a living linguistic treasure, echoed the island's multilayered history, carrying the echoes of Phoenician, Arabic, Italian, and English influences. It served as a bridge that connected us to the heartbeat of the nation.

As the sun set over the horizon, we were captivated by the celestial wonders that have fascinated the Maltese people for millennia. From the ancient observatories of the megalithic temples to the contemporary endeavors in astronomy and space exploration, Malta's fascination with the cosmos is a testament to the human spirit of curiosity and exploration.

In the epilogue of our journey, we stand in awe of Malta's indomitable spirit—a spirit that cherishes its past while embracing the future. It is a spirit that weaves together the threads of heritage, progress, and sustainability, creating a tapestry of promise and possibility. As we bid farewell to this extraordinary island, we carry with us the cherished memories and the sense of wonder that Malta has bestowed upon us.

With grateful hearts, we celebrate Malta—the island of wonders—that has ignited our imagination, enriched our souls, and left an eternal mark on our lives. And though our physical journey may end, our spiritual connection with Malta endures, reminding us that the allure of this captivating land will forever call us back to its embrace.

Farewell, dear Malta, until we meet again. May your future be as bright as your storied past, and may the echoes of your beauty and charm reverberate through the ages. You have given us a treasure trove of memories, and for that, we are forever grateful.

Printed in Great Britain
by Amazon

33826780R00066